Tea Cozies 2

Tea Cozies 2

GUILD OF MASTER CRAFTSMAN PUBLICATIONS

First published 2009 by
Guild of Master Craftsman Publications Ltd
Castle Place, 166 High Street,
Lewes, East Sussex BN7 1XU

Copyright in the Work © GMC Publications Ltd, 2009

Reprinted 2010 (twice)

ISBN 978-1-86108-659-4

Charts and pattern checking by Gina Alton

Associate Publisher: Jonathan Bailey
Production Manager: Jim Bulley
Managing Editor: Gerrie Purcell
Project Editor: Alison Howard
Managing Art Editor: Gilda Pacitti
Design: Rob Janes
Photographer: Laurel Guilfoyle

Set in Gill Sans

Colour origination by GMC Reprographics
Printed and bound in Thailand by KNP

Why we love tea cozies

TEA IS SUCH AN IMPORTANT PART OF EVERYDAY LIFE. Who doesn't look forward to the first cup of tea in the morning, a reviving brew at intervals during the day, or kicking off their shoes after a hard day at work and reaching for the kettle?

The cup that cheers is seen as the panacea for all problems, from exhaustion to bad news. Offering a cup of tea is a gesture of simple friendship, and the ideal way to welcome a visitor. Increasingly, though, making tea just involves dunking a teabag straight into a mug. The teapot is left forlorn at the back of the cupboard, emerging only for tea parties and large gatherings. Yet in other cultures, the act of making tea is treated with great respect; in Japan, the Tea Ceremony is an occasion for great reverence.

We think it's time to dust off the teapot, use it for its intended purpose, and give it the respect it deserves as the iconic centrepiece of an important occasion. And, just as you dress up for an important event, your teapot should also be arrayed in its ceremonial robes in the form of a lovely cozy.

At *Knitting* magazine, we held competitions asking readers to design and make cozies, and they came in thick and fast. 30 designs metamorphosed into the book *Tea Cozies*, but we still had lots more lovely cozies left, and it was only fair to share them. The result is *Tea Cozies 2*, and we hope you will enjoy making them just as much.

Emma Kennedy
Editor
Knitting magazine

Contents

Everything's coming up roses with this gorgeous design by
Rachel Proudman. Why not give someone a beautiful bouquet
that will last far longer than real flowers?

Tea posy

Materials

Debbie Bliss Donegal Aran Tweed (96yds/88m per 50g)

2 x 50g balls Light Green 281111 (A)

2 x 50g balls Pink 281121 (B)

2 x 50 balls Lilac 281107 (C)

A pair of 5mm (US8:UK6) needles

Crochet hook to make chain loop

1 x button

Special techniques

Wrap and turn (W&T): bring yarn to front; slip next st k-wise,
turn. Place slipped st back on right needle. On subsequent
rows, knit the loop along with the slipped st

Tension

17 sts and 24 rows to 4in (10cm) over stocking stitch on
5mm needles before felting;
20 sts and 22 rows to 4in (10cm) after felting

Sides (make 2)

Using 5mm needles and A, cast on 45 sts and work 4 rows g-st.

Beg with a knit row, work 20 rows st st.

Row 1: *(k7, k2tog); rep from * to end (40 sts).

Next and every foll alt row: Purl.

Row 3: K to end.

Row 5: *(k6, k2tog); rep from * to end (35 sts).

Row 7: *(k5, k2tog); rep from * to end (30 sts).

Cont in this way, dec 5 sts on each row, until 10 sts rem.

Row 19: *(k2 tog) to end (5 sts).

Rows 20: Purl.

Break off yarn and thread through rem sts. Draw up and fasten off.

Making up

Join two sides of cozy down one side, leaving a hole for the spout. Join the other side from the top to the top of the handle. Make a chain loop to fit button on one side of the garter stitch lower edge.

Place the cozy in the drum of the washing machine and run through a full cycle at 40°C to felt lightly. Pull gently to shape, and allow to dry completely.

Flowers
(make 17 pink and 14 lilac)

These are formed from a wedge shape made using short row shaping.

Cast on 44 sts and knit 1 row.

Row 1: Knit.

Row 2: K33, W&T.

Row 3: Purl.

Row 4: K23, W&T.

Row 5: Purl.

Row 6: K13, W&T.

Row 7: Purl.

Row 8: K across all sts, picking up the loops below the slipped sts and knitting them with the slipped sts.

Row 9: Purl.

Row 10: K2tog to end (22 sts).

Row 11: P2 tog to end (11 sts).

Break off yarn and draw through rem sts. Finish off ends.

Felt the flowers in the same way as the cozy. While damp, form into spirals with the narrow end of the wedge in the centre. Leave to dry completely on a radiator or in the airing cupboard.

Attaching the flowers and button

Catch the end of the spiral on each flower together and attach to cozy using sewing thread. Attach button to lower edge to corresp with chain loop.

The inspiration for this cozy is that staple of every woman's wardrobe. Charmaine Fletcher incorporated Coco Chanel's love of texture and trademark camellia in this new take on a classic design.

Little black dress

Materials

Hayfield Bonus DK (200m per 100g ball)

1 x 100g ball in 965 Black (M)

Palette DK (348yds/320m per 100g ball)

1 x 100g ball in Cream (C)

20 x 5mm cream pearls and 8 x 4mm cream pearls

1yd (1m) of 1in (2.5cm) wide cream ribbon

A pair each of 4mm (US6:UK8) and 3.25mm (US3:UK10)

bamboo needles; a 3.75mm (US5:UK9) double-pointed needle

Sewing needle and thread; blunt tapestry needle

Dressmaker's pins

Special techniques

Moss stitch

P1tbs/P1tfs: Purl through the back of the (next) st, then purl through the front of this st to increase 'invisibly'

PB: place bead (see instructions)

Tension

20 sts to 4in (10cm) in width, measured over moss stitch on 4mm needles

Placing beads

Take the bead to where it is to be placed, as close to the next st as poss. Slip this st on to the right needle, place the bead, take yarn back and knit the next st. Ensure the bead is positioned over the slipped st, and keep the tension medium to tight to prevent it from working through to the back.

Sides (make 2)

Thread 20 x 5mm pearl beads on to a strand of M, using sewing cotton and a regular needle to assist.

Using the thumb method and 4mm needles cast on 42 sts. Push the beads along the yarn until they are needed.

Row 1: P to end.

Row 2: K to end.

Row 3: P to end.

Row 4: (picot): K2 *(yrn, k2tog), rep from * to last 2 sts, yrn, k2 (43 sts).

Row 5: P to end.

Row 6: K to end.

Row 7: P to end.

Change to C, keeping tension tight if using Palette DK.

Row 8: K to end.

Row 9: K to end. Change to M.

Row 10: K to end.

Row 11: P to end.

Row 12: (bead row): K3, PB on the next st, *(k3, PB); rep from* to last 3 sts, k3.

Row 13: P to end.

Change to C.

Row 14: K to end.

Row 15: K to end.

Change to M.

Row 16: K to end.

Row 17: P1, k1 to end.

Row 18: K1, p1 to end.

Rows 17 and 18 form the moss stitch patt. Rep these two rows until the moss stitch segment measures 6in (15cm), ending on a wrong side row

Eyelet section

Row 1: (RS): K to end.

Row 2: P to end.

Row 3: (eyelet row): K4 *(yrn, k2 tog, k3); rep from *to last 4 sts, yrn, k4 (44 sts).

Row 4: P to end.

Row 5: K to end.

Moss stitch section

Row 1: P1 k1 to end.

Row 2: K1 p1 to end.

These two rows form the moss stitch pattern; rep for a further 18 rows until this new moss stitch segment measures 2in (5cm), ending with a RS row. Cast off.

Camellia

Note: working the dec 1 st in from the edge gives the flower its characteristic curved petal. Leave long tails at the beg and end for assembly and stitching.

Using 3.25mm needles and thumb method, cast on 2 sts.

Row 1: K2.

Row 2: P1, p1tbs, p1tfs (3 sts).

Row 3: K to end.

Row 4: P1, p1tbs, p1tfds (4 sts).

Row 5: K to end.

Row 6: P1, p1tbs, p1tfs (5 sts).

Row 7: K to end.

Row 8: P1, p1tbs, p1tfs (6 sts).

Row 9: K to end.

Row 10: P1, p1tbs, p1tfs (7 sts).

Row 11: K to end.

Row 12: P1, p1tbs, p1tfs (8 sts).

Row 13: K to end.

Row 14: P to end.

Row 15: K to end.

Row 16: P to end.

Row 17: K to end.

Row 18: P1, p2tog, p5 (7 sts).

Row 19: K to end.

Row 20: P1, p2 tog, p4 (6 sts).
Row 21: K to end.
Row 22: P1, p2tog, p3 (5 sts).
Row 23: K5 to end.
Row 24: P1, p2tog, p2 (4 sts).
Row 25: K to end.
Row 26: P1, p2tog, p1 (3 sts).
Row 27: K to end.
Row 28: P1, p2tog (2 sts).
Row 29: K2 to end.
Rep rows 2–29 three times more
(4 petals in all).
Cast off, leaving two long tails.

Stamen

Using two 3.75 double-pointed needles,
cast on 6 sts. Knit a row, but do not
turn. With yarn at back, push sts along
needle and knit them again. Rep until
work measures approx 1½in (4cm).
Cut yarn, leaving a long tail. Thread tail
on a darning needle. Thread through
rem sts and draw together very gently
to keep the top stitches tidy. Draw the
darning needle down through the
middle of these stitches and unthread.
Neaten and fasten off cast–off row.

Making up
Camellia

With the work on its side, thread
through the first row of sts along the
end opposite curved petals, gathering
and overlapping as necessary to
produce flower effect. Fasten off but
do not cut yarn. Using cast-on tail,
work along the same row in the
opposite direction to pull the flower
centre even closer together. Fasten
off but do not cut yarn. Place stamen
in centre of flower, bend to the left
and secure to the first petal on left
using one of the tail threads; do not
cut thread. Split one of the tail threads,
and thread one of the sections on a
regular needle. Manoeuvre to lower
left side of the right petal thus: attach
a 4mm bead; rep until 8 beads form a
semi-circle at the bottom of the
stamen. Fasten off and cut. Take rem
tail back and forth 2 or 3 times
across centre back of flower to form
a short loop. Neaten loop using
buttonhole stitch and fasten off.

Cozy

Join sides using mattress stitch, leaving
gaps for handle and spout. Leave a gap
in each seam of eyelet row to form two
extra eyelets. Fasten off. Thread ribbon
through, beg at centre eyelet on right
side. Draw up and form a bow. Loop the
right-hand ribbon and thread through
loop on back of flower. Turn cozy upside-
down and finish tying bow so the ribbon
tails face the bottom of cozy. Trim ribbon
and coat ends with clear nail varnish to
prevent fraying.

Tip

*Make sure the ribbon
matches the cream yarn
exactly, as any variation will
make the yarn look 'dirty'.*

This amazing woodland fantasy by Gina Woodward
is not nearly as complicated as it looks – all the mushrooms
are worked separately and sewn on!

Magic mushrooms

Materials

Rowan Pure Wool DK (127yds/125m per 50g ball)

1 x 50g ball blue (B)

Small amounts of the same yarn in green (G), cream (C),
red (R), mustard (M), tan (T) and orange (O)

Rowan Pure Wool 4-ply

1 x 50g ball in cream for lining

Small amounts in dark purple, orange and gunmetal grey

A pair each of 3.75mm (US5:UK9)and 2.75mm (US2:UK12)
straight needles; a pair of 2.75mm double-pointed needles

A stitch holder or spare needle

Special techniques

Intarsia

Stocking stitch

Making an I-cord

Stalks (see pattern instructions)

Kt (knot): cast on 2 sts, cast off 2 sts, all into same st

Tension

22 sts and 40 rows to 4in (10cm) over stocking stitch in
DK using 3.75mm. needles

Note: As there are so many colours, generic names have been used for yarn shades. This will make it easier if you want to substitute yarn.

Working the stalks

Where marked on the chart, work the stalk st separately for 4 further rows and fasten off, leaving a long yarn end to attach it inside the cluster of the mushroom. To take its place, pick up the next st from the row below and knit into the back.

Side 1

Using 3.75mm needles and B, cast on 56 sts and work 3 rows st st.

Next row (WS): Knit.

Beg with a k row, work 4 rows in st st.

Next row (form hem): K each st along row tog with its corresponding st on cast-on edge.

Next row: Purl.

Join in G and work 2 rows st st.

Now work chart A.

Break off yarn and leave sts on a holder.

Side 2

Work as for side 1, working chart B in place of chart A. Do not break off yarn.

Next row: L across all 56 sts, then across 56 sts of side 1 (112 sts).

Next row: P across all sts.

Shape top

Row 1: *(k5, k2tog); rep from * to end.

Row 2 and foll alt rows: Purl.

Row 3: *(k4, k2tog); rep from * to end.

Cont to dec in this way until there are 32 sts on needle, ending with a purl row.

Eyelets

Next row: K1, *(yf, k2tog); rep from * to last st, k1.

Beg with a purl row, work 8 rows st st.

Next row: (WS): Knit.

Break off B and join in R. Beg with a knit row, work 8 rows in st st, making 6kt in C at random along each of rows 3, 5 and 7.

Cast off in R, leaving a long end. Use this to catch down the 8 rows worked in R to form a hem just above eyelet holes.

Cluster bell mushroom

Make 4 in orange 4-ply and 5 in dark purple 4-ply.

Using 2.75mm needles, cast on 12 sts and work 4 rows in st st.

Row 5: (sl1, k1, psso) 6 times (6 sts). Cut yarn, leaving a long end. Thread through rem sts, draw up and fasten side seam.

Horn of plenty mushroom

Make 1 of each size, foll instructions in brackets for size variations.

Using 3.75mm double-pointed needles and grey 4-ply, cast on 2 sts.

Work the next rows using the I-cord technique as folls:

Next row (RS): K2, *(push both sts to opp end of needle. Without turning, knit sts again, taking yarn tightly across back of work).

Rep from * 4(6:8) times.

Next row: Inc in each st, turn (4 sts).

Next row: Purl.

Next row: K, inc at both ends of row. Rep last 2 rows 1(2:4) times (8[10:14] sts).

Next row: Purl.

Next row: K0(1:2) sts, *(k into front, back, then front again of next st); rep from * to last 0(1:2) sts, k0(1:2) sts (24 [26:34] sts).

Next row: Cast off, leaving a long end.

Mushroom tassels
(make 2)

Using 2.75mm needles and R, cast on 20 sts and work 2 rows st st.

Next row: (WS) Knit.

Beg with a knit row, work 4 further rows st st.

Next row (form hem): Knit each st tog with its corresp st on cast-on edge.

Next row: Purl.

Magic mushroom chart *56 sts x 36 rows*

Each square = 1 st and 1 row

Read RS rows from R to L and WS rows from L to R

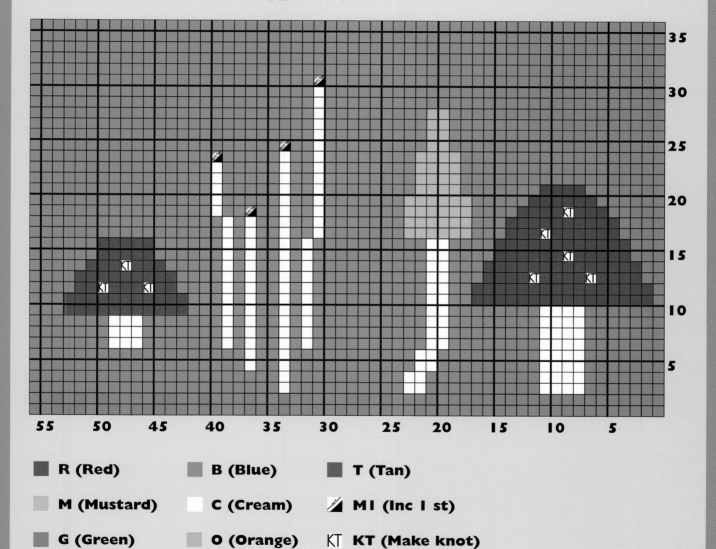

R (Red)   B (Blue)   T (Tan)

M (Mustard)   C (Cream)   M1 (Inc 1 st)

G (Green)   O (Orange)   KT (Make knot)

Next row: Knit, making kt in C in sts 5,10,15 and 20.
Rep last 2 rows, but make kt in C in sts 2,7,12 and 17.
Next row: Purl.
Next row: (k2tog) to end.
Next row: (p2tog) to end (5 sts).
Break off yarn and thread through rem sts. Draw up, and sew down side seam.

Cord

Using double-pointed 2.75mm needles and C, cast on 4 sts and knit 1 row.
Work in I-cord over all 4 sts for a further 9 rows.
Next row: (k2tog) twice.
Break off C and join in B.
Cont for approx 18in (36cm).
Attach mushroom tassels by threading a tassel on to the cord, then passing it

through the eyelets, meeting at centre of chart A. Thread the second tassel on to the cord. Break off B and cont in C.
Next row: Inc in both sts.
Work a further 9 rows of I-cord.
Next row: (k2tog) twice, sl first st over second st.
Fasten off.

Lining (make 2)

Using 3.75mm needles and cream 4-ply, cast on 48 sts and work in st st for 36 rows. Cast off.

Making up

Join side seams of cozy, leaving gaps for handle and spout. Join back seams of Horn of Plenty mushrooms and attach to cozy. Attach each cluster bell mushroom immediately above its stalk. Thread stalk extension inside bell and secure. Sew both pieces of lining to cozy, covering area from hem to start of top shaping. Sew in ends.

Magic mushroom chart (alternative) *56 sts x 36 rows*

Each square = I st and I row

Read RS rows from R to L and WS rows from L to R

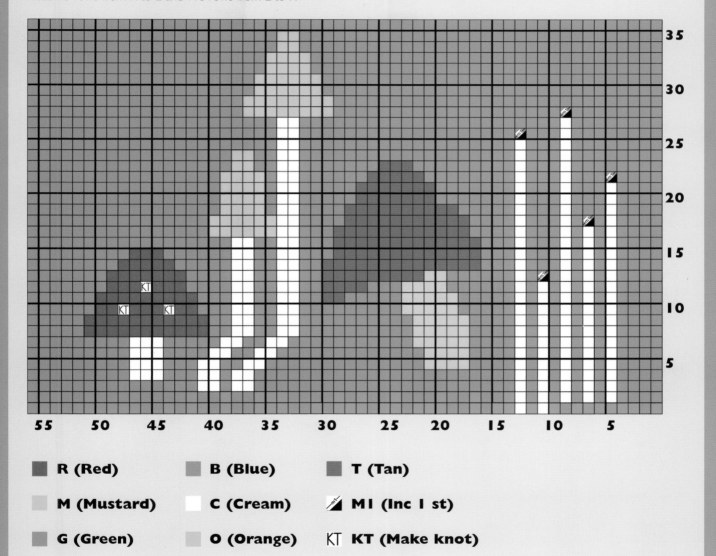

R (Red) B (Blue) T (Tan)

M (Mustard) C (Cream) MI (Inc I st)

G (Green) O (Orange) KT KT (Make knot)

This simple tea cosy in mistake rib by Frankie Brown is quick to knit and shown in two variations. Aran-weight yarn makes a cozy to fit a six-cup pot, but the pattern can be adapted for another size by changing the yarn.

Mistake rib

Materials

Any Aran-weight yarn

1 x 50g ball

A pair of 4.5mm (US7:UK7) needles

Sewing needle and thread for beading

Blunt tapestry needle

Dressmaker's pins

Clear nail polish (optional)

Special techniques

Mistake rib (see instrucctions)

Tension

20 sts and 26 rows to 4in (10cm) over stocking stitch on 4.5mm needles

Sides (make 2)

Cast on 31 sts and set rib patt as folls:

Row 1: P2, k2 to last 3 sts, p2, k1.

Row 2: Rep first row.

Work 4 rows, inc 1 st at beg of each and taking incs into patt as set (35 sts).

Next row: K2, p2 to last 3 sts, k2, p1.

Work 29 more rows in mistake rib.

Shape top

Row 1: (K2, p2, k1, p2tog, p1) 4 times, k2, p1 (31sts).

Row 2: (K2, p2, k1, p2) 4 times, k2, p1.

Row 3: (K2, p2, k1, p2tog) 4 times, k2, p1 (27 sts).

Row 4: (K2, p1, k1, p2) 4 times, k2, p1.

Row 5: (K2, p2, k2tog) 4 times, k2, p1 (23 sts).

Row 6: (K2, p3) 4 times, k2, p1.

Row 7: K2 (p2, k2tog, k1) 4 times, p1 (19 sts).

Tip

If you prefer to leave the lid of your pot uncovered, cast off after row 2 of the top shaping.

Row 8: K2, p2 to last 3 sts, k2, p1.

Row 9: (K2, p2tog) 4 times, p2, p1 (15 sts).

Row 10: K2, p1 across row.

Row 11: K1, p2tog across row (10 sts).

Row 12: K1, p1 across row.

Cast off loosely in rib.

This completes one side of the cozy. Make another to match.

Making up

Join each piece 1½in (4cm) up from lower edge and 2½in (6cm) from top for spout seam and 2in (5cm) up from lower edge and 4in (10cm) from top for handle seam. These measurements are approximate; try the cozy on the teapot and adjust as necessary before fastening off.

Variation

For a smaller (three-cup) teapot foll the same instructions using DK yarn and 3.75mm (US9:US5) needles. Join for 1in (2.5cm) at lower edge and 2in (5cm) at top for handle seam, and ¾in (2cm) at lower edge and 2½in (6cm) at top for spout seam.

This ingenious design by Vikki Harding uses variegated yarn to produce a stunning but simple Fairisle pattern. The I-cord drawstring and tassels add a quirky finishing touch.

Fairisle

Materials

Wild Fire Fibres Jupiter Merino Aran (188yds/170m per 100g)

1 x 100g skein Fresh Berries

Rowan Pure Wool Aran (186yds/169m per 100g)

1 x 100g skein black

A pair of 5mm (US8:UK6) bamboo needles

2 x 5mm (US8:UK6) double-pointed needles for I-cord

A 4.5mm (US7:UK7) crochet hook

Special techniques

Fairisle

Making an I-cord

Measurements

25cm high x 45cm in circumference

Tension

22 sts and 20 rows to 4in (10cm) over pattern using 5mm needles

Sides (make 2)

Using M, cast on 40 sts and foll chart, working 1 st in M at beg and end of each row. Rep chart across every row.

Row 26: Using M, p across, dec 4 sts evenly across row (36 sts).

Row 27: Knit all sts.

Row 28: P2tog, p to centre st, p2tog, p to last 2 sts, p2tog (33 sts).

Row 29: Using M, k2tog, k to centre st, k2tog, k to last 2 sts, k2tog (30 sts).

Row 30: Using M, p across.

Row 31: K2tog, k to centre st, k2tog, k to last 2 sts, k2tog (27 sts).

Row 32: Using M, p across.

Row 33: Using M, k2tog, k to centre st, k2tog, k to last 2 sts, k2tog (24 sts).

Row 34: Using M, p2tog, p to centre st, p2tog, p to last 2 sts, p2tog (21 sts).

Row 35: Using M, k2tog, k to centre st, k2tog, k to last 2 sts, k2tog (18 sts).

Row 36: Using M, purl across.

Row 37 (eyelets): K1, *(yo, k2tog); rep from * to end of row.

Row 38: P across.

Row 39–40: Work rows 3 and 4 of chart across these 18 sts.

Rows 41–48: Using M, work in st st. Cast off using C.

Lower edge

Using M, pick up the 18 cast-off sts at the top of each piece from the inside of sts, as the crochet will fold down inside the piece. Work 8 rows dc.

Making up

Join the sides, leaving holes for spout and handle. Sew in ends of yarn. Sew crocheted top hem down on inside.

Finishing

Using M, pick up the sts around the spout hole and work 2 rows dc. Pick up sts round handle hole and work a row of dc. Work a second row of dc, dec 12 sts evenly across row. Pick up the sts round lower edge and, using M, work 4 rows dc. Sew this hem up on the inside to form a neat, thick edge that will prevent the work from curling.

> ## Tip
>
> *Take care not to pull the yarn too tightly across the back of the work when working in Fairisle.*

Making an I-cord

Using M, cast on 3 sts and work in I-cord for 18in (45cm). Thread through the eyelet holes. Make two thick tassels using both yarns and attach to ends.

Fairisle chart *40 sts x 25 rows*

Each square = 1 st and 1 row

Read RS rows from R to L and WS rows from L to R

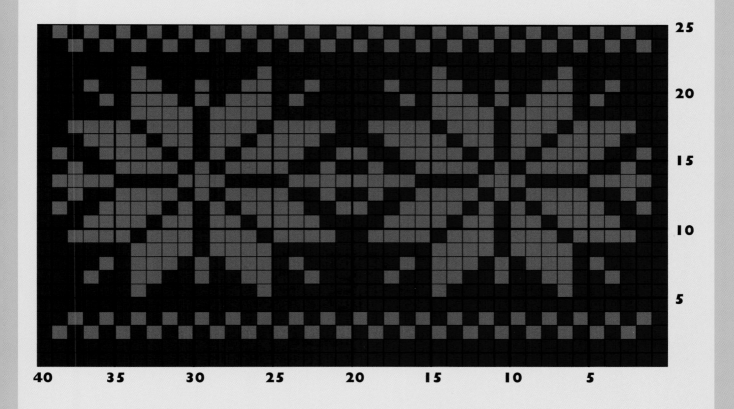

 M

 C

Tea and cakes are a perfect combination, and this simple yet mouthwatering design by Nicola Haisley is inspired by a teatime favourite – it should tempt you to get out the knitting needles.

Battenberg slice

Materials

James C Brett Top Value Double Knitting
1 x 100g ball Lemon 8412 (M)
1 x 100g ball Pink 8421 (C)
A pair of 5.5mm (US9:UK5) needles

Tension

8 sts and 11 rows to 4in (10cm) over stocking stitch using 5.5mm needle and double yarn, unstretched

Main body (make 2)

Using M double, cast on 24 sts and work two rows in g-st.

Working the squares

Row 1: Using M, k12. Join in C and k to end.

Row 2: P12 in C, pick up M, p to end. Rep these 2 rows 6 times more.

Next row: Using M, knit.

Next row: Using M, p12. Pick up C and p to end.

Next row: Using C, k12. Pick up A and k to end.

Rep the last 2 rows 4 times more.

Working the decreases

Keeping the square patt as set, dec 1 st at each end of next 5 rows, using shaped decs (14 sts).

Cast off knitwise.

Marzipan trim (make 2)

Using A, cast on 3 sts and work 110 rows in g-st.

Cast off.

Making up

Sew the marzipan strip round the outside edge of the cozy (excluding the bottom), stretching gently if necessary. Join both sides, leaving room for the spout and handle.

The cup and saucer on top of this design by Diane Dowgill will be a real talking point, and it's lined for extra insulation. It's the ideal accessory for traditional blue and white pottery.

Cornish ware

Materials

Sirdar Supersoft Aran (236m per 100g)

1 x 100g ball blue (M)

Any Aran-weight yarn

Approx 30g white (C)

A 4.5mm (US7:UK7) circular needle approximately 16in (40cm) long

A pair of 4.5mm (US7:UK7) straight needles

Set of 5 x 4.5mm (US7:UK7) needles

Pipe cleaner or short length of fine wire to stiffen cup handle

Special techniques

MB: make bobble (see instructions)

Striped rib (see instructions)

Tension

19.5 sts and 28 rows to 4in (10cm) over stocking stitch on 4.5mm needles

Body – worked in one piece

Using the circular needle and M, cast on 100 sts and work in rounds.

Rounds 1–5: *(K1C, p1M); rep from * to end to form striped rib.

Rounds 6–7: Knit, using M.

Round 8: MB in 2nd and every foll 4th st to end (25 bobbles).

Make bobble

Into next st: k1, k1tbl, k1, k1tbl, k1, turn.

Next row: K5, turn.

Next row: K5, turn.

Next row: (K2tog) twice, k1, turn.

Next row: K3tog tbl.

Round 9: Knit, using M.

Rounds 10–13: Knit, using C.

Divide for handle and spout

The sides are now worked separately using stocking stitch and straight needles.

Next row: Using M, k50, leave rem sts on spare length of yarn.

Work a further 23 rows in stripe patt (4 rows M, 4 rows C), carrying yarn not in use up side of work.

Break off yarn, rejoin to other side and complete to match.

Join for top

Begin working using the circular needle, changing to the double-pointed needles when necessary.

Next round: Using the circular needle and M. work across both sides (00 sts).

Work 3 rows in M.

Shape top

Round 1: Using C, work to end.

Round 2: (k8, k2tog) to end (90 sts).

Round 3 and alt rounds: Knit.

Round 4: (k7, k2tog) to end (80 sts).

Cont as set until the row '(k3, k3tog) to end' has been worked (40 sts).

Break off C and cont in A only.

Saucer

Round 1: Purl.

Rounds 2 and 3: Knit.

Round 4: (k2tog, yrn) to end.

Round 5: Knit, working all yrn sts.

Round 6 and 7: Knit.

Round 8: Purl.

Round 9 and alt rounds: Knit.

Round 10: (k2, k2tog) to end (30 sts).

Round 12: (k1, k2tog) to end (20 sts).

Round 14: K2tog to end (10 sts).

Round 16: K2tog to end (5 sts).

Break off yarn and thread end through these 5 sts. Pull up tightly and secure.

Teacup

Using M and leaving a tail approx 6in (15cm) long, cast on 24 sts and work 4 rows of striped rib as for sides.

Break off C and cont in M only.

Work 2 rows in stocking stitch.

Next row: Knit, MB as before in sts 2, 5, 8, 11, 14, 17, 20 and 23.

Work 3 rows in st st.

Cast off.

Lining

Using A and the circular needle, cast on 96 sts and work 8 rows in the round. Change to straight needles and work 24 rows stocking stitch on first 48 sts only. Complete second side to match.

Next round: Resume working all the round and knit 6 rows across all sts.

Top shaping

Round 1: (k6, k2tog) to end (84 sts).

Round 2 and alt rounds: Knit.

Round 3: (k5, k2tog) to end (72 sts).

Round 5: (k4, k2tog) to end (60 sts).

Round 7: (k3, k2tog,) to end (48 sts).

Round 9: (k2, k2tog,) to end (36 sts).

Round 11: (k2tog) to end (18 sts).

Cast off.

Making up

Sew in ends. Join side seam of teacup. With RS of work facing, place the two purl rows of the saucer tog and stitch through carefully so the 'yrn' sts form a picot edge. Turn cozy inside out and place lining inside, WS tog. Pin the two pieces together at spout and handle openings. Sew lower edge of lining in place just above ribbing and at top saucer edge. Join lining and main piece at spout and handle openings. Turn work RS out and, working from the inside of the cup, attach securely to top of cozy.

Strands of green and white yarn worked together give the effect of a misty spring morning in this design by Sheila Woolrich. The leaves and flowers are worked separately and sewn on when the cover is complete.

Spring

Materials

Any DK yarn

1 x 100g ball green (M)

1 x 50g ball white (C)

Oddments of yellow and pink

A pair of 5.5mm (US9:UK5) needles

A pair of 4mm (US6:UK8) needles

A 3.25mm (USD/3:UK10) crochet hook

Narrow ribbon for bows

Special techniques

Garter stitch

Garter stitch rib pattern (see instructions)

Tension

Not critical as garter stitch rib pattern is very stretchy

Sides (make 2)

Cast on 29 sts using 5.5mm needles and work in patt for 40 rows.

Next row: K to end.

Next row: *(p1, k3); rep from * to last st, p1.

Shape top

Next row: K3*(k2tog, k2); rep from * to end (22 sts).

Next row: *(p1, k2); rep from * to last st, p1.

Next row: K2, *(k2tog, k1); rep from * to end (15 sts).

Next row: *(p1, k1); rep from * to end, p1.

Next row: K1, *(k2tog); rep from * to end (8 sts).

Break yarn and thread through rem sts. Fasten off.

Leaves (make 16)

Using 4mm needles and one strand of green yarn, cast on 2 sts.

Next row: Inc 1, k to end.

Rep last row until there are 8 sts.

Work 8 rows in g-st.

Next row: Sl1, k1, psso.

Rep last row until 2 sts rem.

Next row: K2tog.

Fasten off.

Large crochet flower

Using yellow yarn, make 6ch and join into ring using a ss.

Round 1: Work (1 dc, 3ch) six times into ring. Join to first dc using a ss. Change to pink yarn.

Round 2: Ss into first 3-ch sp. Work (1dc, 3ch, 3tr, 3ch, 1dc) into each space. Join to first dc using a ss. Fasten off.

Chain flower base

Using green yarn, make 10ch and ss into first ch to form a loop.

Repeat until there are five loops. Join using a ss and fasten off.

Small crochet flower

Using pink yarn, make a ring round finger and work (2ch, 2tr, 2ch, 1ss) five times into. Join using a ss and fasten off. Pull starting thread into a tight ring and fasten off.

Making up

Join both sides of cover for 1¼in (3cm). Leave a 2¼in (5.5cm) gap for handle and spout. Join rem seam on either side.

Layer eight of the leaves and the large crochet flower and attach to top of cover as shown. Join the six small crochet flowers to the flower bases. Arrange the flowers and the rest of the leaves to the cover as shown. Finish off with two small double ribbon bows.

Tip

Follow the arrangement of leaves and flowers shown or create your own design.

This design by Jean Costello is ideal for using up odd balls of yarn. Crocheting rows over a strand of contrast yarn creates a subtle two-tone effect and gives the work extra body.

Tapestry

Materials

Any DK yarn

1 x 25g ball blue

1 x 25g ball pink

1 x 25g ball yellow

Oddment of green

4.5mm (US7:UK7) crochet hook

3.5mm (USE/4: UK9) crochet hook

Special techniques

French knots

Tapestry crochet: see instructions

Measurements

Cover measures approximately 6½in (16.5cm) high

Tension

Approximately 8 trebles to 2in (5cm) in width

Sides (make 2)

Using the 4.5mm hook and green yarn, make 42ch.

Row 1: Work 1dc into each ch, turn.

Row 2: 2ch, work 1dc into each ch, turn. Break off green.

Note: these two rows will be unravelled later to form the frill.

Row 3: Using pink and yellow tog, work 1dc into each dc of previous row, turn. Break off pink and join in green; carry yellow up side of work.

Row 4: Using green, work 1dc into each ch, turn.

Break off green and join in blue.

Row 5: Using blue, make 3ch, work 1tr into each dc of the previous row. *At the same time* run the yellow along the top of the previous row at the front, trapping it as you work the blue trebles.

Row 6: Rep row 5.

Row 7: Rep row 5.

Row 8: Using yellow, make 2ch, work 1dc into each space. *At the same time* run the blue yarn along the top of the previous row at the front, working the yellow dc sts over the blue. Rep rows 5–8 once, then rep row 5 again.

Note: For a taller cozy, work one or two extra rows of trebles in blue with yellow running through at this point.

Shape top

Next row: Using the 3.5mm hook and yellow with blue running through, work 1dc in each sp of previous row. Cont across second piece to join sides, and join into a round with a ss.

Next round: Using yellow with blue running through, work 1dc into *every other* sp of previous round; join with a ss.

Next round: Using yellow with blue running through, work 1htr into each sp of previous round, join with a ss.

Next round: Using yellow with blue running through, work 1htr into *every other* sp of previous round, join with a ss.

Next round: Using yellow, work 1htr into every sp of previous round, join with ss.

Next round: Using pink and yellow tog, work (3 htr, 3ch) into every space of previous row.

Next round: Using pink, work (3htr, 3ch) into every space at the base of the previous round. Fasten off.

Make another piece the same, but do not break off yarn.

Central circle

Using yellow, make 5ch and join into a ring using a ss.

Next round: Work (3 htr, 3ch) five times into ring. Fasten off.

Small flowers
(make 4 pink, 2 yellow)

Make 5ch and join into a ring using a ss. Work as many dc as will fit into the ring, join using a ss.

Next round: Work (1dc, 1ch) into each dc of previous round. Fasten off.

Forming the frill

Unpick the first two rows of crochet (worked in green). This will produce an attractive pink and yellow frill round the lower edge.

Making up

Pull last strand of blue yarn at top of cozy to fit circumference of central circle and create the double frill effect. Fasten off. Sew central circle in place. Attach small flowers as shown, working a contrasting French knot in the centre of each. Using yellow, work 2 rows of dc round spout and handle edges. Join sides for approx 1in (2.5cm). Fasten off and sew in end of yarn.

Tip

The yarn that is carried up the side of the work will be hidden by the crocheted edging.

The red and grey of this tea cozy reminded designer Frankie Brown of school uniforms. The slip stitch tweed pattern is easy to knit and very satisfying as horizontal stripes of colour magically turn into vertical stripes.

School tweed

Materials

Sirdar Country Style DK (348yds/318m per 100g)
25g grey 408 (M)
25g red 402 (C)
A pair of 3.25mm (US3:UK10) needles
A pair of 4mm (US6:UK8) needles

Special techniques

Sl1p-wise wyib: slip 1 st purlwise with yarn held at the back of work
Sl1p-wise wyif: slip 1 st purlwise with yarn held at the front of work
Slip stitch tweed pattern: see instructions

Tension

11 sts and 15 rows to 4in (10cm) in stocking stitch using 4mm needles

Sides (make 2)

Using 3.25mm needles and M, cast on 40 sts and work 9 rows in k2, p2 rib.

Next row: Rib 4, *(m1, rib 2); rep from * to last 2 sts, rib 2 (57 sts).

Change to 4mm needles and knit 1 row. Now foll the 4-row pattern, working 2 rows red and 2 rows grey alternately.

Slip stitch tweed pattern

Row 1: Using C, k2, *(sl1p-wise wyib, k3); rep from * to last 3 sts, sl1p-wise wyib, k2.

Row 2: Using C, k2, *(sl1p-wise wyif, k3); rep from * to last 3 sts, sl1 p-wise wyif, k2.

Row 3: Using A, k4, *(sl1p-wise wyib, k3); rep from * to last st, k1.

Row 4: Using A, k4, *(sl1p-wise wyif, k3); rep from * to last st, k1.

Work 12 reps of patt in total. Change to 3.25mm needles and M only.

Next row: Knit, dec 1 st in the centre of row (56 sts).

Work 10 rows in k2, p2 rib.

Next row: *(k2tog, p2tog), rep from * to end (28 sts).

Work 5 rows in k1, p1 rib.

Next row: *(k2tog), rep from * to end (14 sts).

Change to C for the last few rows.

Next row: P2, *(p2tog, p1); rep from * to end (10 sts).

Beg with a purl row, work 5 rows in reverse stocking stitch.

Cast off knitwise loosely, using a 4mm needle.

Making up

Join 1¼in (3cm) at the lower edge and 2½in (6cm) at the top for the handle seam. Join 1in (2.5cm) up from lower edge and 4in (10cm) at the top for the spout seam. These are approximate measurements; try the cozy on the teapot and adjust as necessary before fastening off. When joining the halves of the cozy allow the red strip at the top to curl over before sewing down.

Take a break from your chores to enjoy a refreshing cuppa from a pot clad in this cheery design by Ally Howard – it's sure to give you the energy to finish pegging out the laundry!

Washday

Materials

Twilley's Freedom Spirit (131yds/120m per 50g)

1 x 50g ball Nature 514 (A)

Any DK yarn

1 x 25g ball brown (B)

Paton's Fairytale Colour 4 Me

1 x 50g ball New Blue 4988 (C)

Oddment of DK yarn for flowers

Oddments of 2- or 3-ply yarn in various shades for clothes

A pair of 5mm (US8:UK6) needles

A pair of 3.25mm (US3:UK10) needles

Special techniques

Garter stitch

French knots

Tension

13 sts to 4in (10cm) in width over stocking stitch on 5mm needles, using main yarn double

Note: yarns A, B and C are used double throughout. Before you begin, divide each into two smaller balls, then wind one strand of each together on one ball.

Sides (make 2)

Using yarn A double, cast on 28 sts and work 4 rows in g-st.

Next row: Inc in first st, k to last st, inc1 (30 sts).

Work a further 6 rows in g-st. Do not break off A.

Change to B and work 2 rows st st.

Next row: K4A, *(k2B, k3A); rep to last st, k1.

Next row: K2A, p1A, *(p1B, p1A, p1B, p2A); rep from * to last 2 sts, k2.

Keeping 2-st g-st border correct, work 2 rows in st st.

Change to C and work 14 rows st st. Break off yarn and leave sts on a holder. Complete second side to the same point but do not break off yarn.

Join for top

Next row: K across sts on second side then k across all sts on first side (60 sts).

Next row: Purl.

Next row: (k4, skpo) to end (50 sts).

Next row: Purl.

Next row: (k3, skpo) to end (40 sts).

Next row: Purl.

Next row: (k2, skpo) to end (30 sts).

Next row: Purl.

Next row: (k1, skpo) to end (20 sts).

Next row: Purl.

Next row: (skpo) to end (10 sts).

Next row: Purl.

Next row: Inc in every st (20 sts).

Work 5 rows in st st.

Cast off.

Making up

Join from the top down to the beg of the 2-st g-st border, allowing the last few rows of the top edge to roll down and expose the reverse stocking stitch on the wrong side. Join the first 4 rows of g-st at the lower edge.

Embroidery

Work French knots to represent flowers randomly in contrast yarn.

Jumper
Body (worked in 1 piece to armholes)

Using 3.25mm needles and an oddment of fine random-dyed yarn, cast on 16 sts and work 12 rows in g-st.

Next row: K2 tog, k4, k2tog, turn. Work 5 rows in g-st on the first set of sts only (6 sts), then cast off. Rejoin yarn and work 5 rows g-st on the second set of sts.

Sleeves (make 2)

Cast on 6 sts and work 14 rows g-st.

Next row: K2 tog, k2, k2tog (4 sts). Work 5 rows in g-st on these 5 sts. Cast off.

To finish off

Beg at the dec row, join tops of sleeves to body of jumper. Join side seam.

T-shirt

Using smaller needles, cast on 8 sts.
Work 1 row k1, p1 rib, then 8 rows st st.
Next row: Cast on 3, k to end (11 sts).
Next row: Cast on 3, k to end (14 sts).
Work 4 rows in st st.
Next row: K5, cast off 4, k5.
Next row: K5, cast on 4 sts, k to end.
Work 4 rows in st st.
Next row: Cast off 3 sts, k to end.
Next row: Cast off 3 sts, k to end.
Work 8 rows st st, then 1 row k1, p1 rib.
Cast off.
To finish off
Join side and sleeve seams.

Knickers

Using 3.25mm needles and an oddment of fine yarn, cast on 8 sts and work 4 rows in g-st.
Next row: Dec1, k to end.
Rep last row 3 times (4 sts).
Work 6 rows in g-st.
Next row: Inc in first st, k to end.
Rep last row 3 times (8 sts).
Work 4 rows in g-st.
Cast off, leaving a long end.
To finish off
Join first side seam, then use long end to work blanket stitch round leg opening. Join second side seam and finish leg opening as before.

Camisole

Using smaller needles and an oddment of fine yarn, cast on 8 sts and work 15 rows in g-st.
Next row: (k1, inc in next st) to end.
Cast off.
To finish off
Join side seam. Work tiny loops for straps and blanket stitch over them. Thread contrast yarn through the top of the camisole just below the cast-off stitches, and finish with a French knot

Tea towel

Using smaller needles and an oddment of fine yarn, cast on 9 sts.
Work 2 rows in g-st.
Join in contrast and work 2 rows g-st.
Using main shade, work 16 rows in st st.
Join in contrast and work 2 rows in g-st.
Using main, work 2 rows g-st.
Cast off and sew in ends.

Mini-skirt

Using smaller needles and an oddment of fine yarn, cast on 16 sts.
Knit 2 rows.
Next row: K4, pick up loop bet sts and k into back of it to inc, k8, pick up loop and inc as before, k4 (18 sts).
Next row: Purl.
Next row: K4, inc in next st, k10, inc in next st, k4 (20 sts).
Next row: Purl.
Next row: K5, pick up loop between sts and k into back of it to inc, k10, pick up loop and inc as before, k5 (22 sts).
Next row: Purl.
Knit 2 rows.
Cast off.
To finish off
Join back seam.

Assembling the cozy

Place cozy on pot. Make a twisted cord using fine yarn and arrange in a circle at the top, just below where the shaping starts. Arrange the washing as desired and pin in place – if you do not press the small items they will retain a bit of movement just like washing on a line. Work pegs using small contrasting upright stitches to fasten items on line. Catch-stitch items in place from reverse.

This ultra-simple design by Lucy Norris incorporates a heartfelt sentiment. Ring the changes and show someone how much you care by substituting their initial for the 'T'.

I love T

Materials

Rowan Handknit DK
1 x 50g ball in Linen 205 (M)
Oddments of same yarn in Black 252 (B) and Rosso 215 (R)
A pair of 4.5mm (US7:UK7) needles

Special techniques

Garter stitch
Intarsia

Tension

18 sts measure 4in (10cm) in width over stocking stitch on 4.5mm needles

Body (worked in one piece until end of rib)

Using M, cast on 82 sts and work 8 rows in g-st for lower edge.

Row 1: K41, turn leaving rem sts on holder. Work on these 41 sts for first side.

Row 2: k2, p to last 2 sts, k2.

Rows 3–8: Work in stocking stitch, keeping a 2-st g-st border at the end of every row.

Rows 9–14: Work motif from chart.

Rows 15–21: As rows 3–8, ending on a knit row.

Transfer sts from holder to needle, then place sts from first side on holder.

Work 21 rows in stocking stitch, keeping a 2-st g-st border at the end of every row.

Next row: P40, k1.

Transfer 41 sts from holder to needle; k1, p40 on these sts.

Next RS row: K1,* (k6, k2tog); rep from * to last st, k1.

Next and alt rows (WS): P all sts.

Next RS row: K1,* (k5, k2tog); rep from * to last st, k1.

Next RS row: K1,* (k4, k2tog); rep from * to last st, k1.

Next RS row: K1,* (k3, k2tog); rep from * to last st, k1.

Next RS row: K1,* (k2, k2tog); rep from * to last st, k1.

Next RS row: K1,* (k1, k2tog); rep from * to last st, k1.

Next RS row: K1, *(k2tog); rep from * to last st, k1.

Loop yarn through rem st and pull tight.

Making up

Join top and bottom seam. Sew in ends.

Tip

Work intarsia motifs using small balls of yarn, and do not carry sts across back of work.

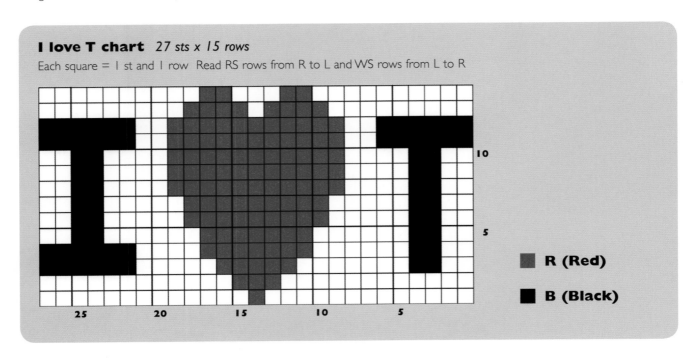

I love T chart *27 sts x 15 rows*

Each square = 1 st and 1 row Read RS rows from R to L and WS rows from L to R

■ R (Red)

■ B (Black)

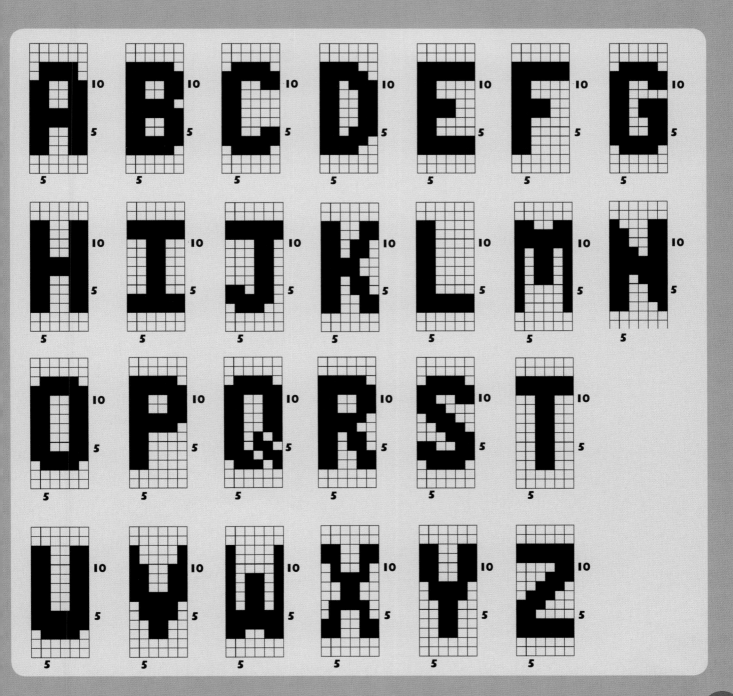

Sometimes you really do want no fuss, no frills and no decorations. This simple design in chunky yarn from Sarah Cox is an ideal bazaar item or a gift for anyone who prefers the minimalist look.

No frills

Materials

Any chunky yarn or DK yarn (used double)
Approx 50g red
A pair of 5mm (US8:UK6) needles

Tension

15 sts measure 4in (10cm) in width over stocking stitch on 5mm needles

Sides (make 2)

Cast on 31 sts and work 4 rows in g-st. Now work in st st with a 2-st g-st border thus:

Row 1: K across.

Row 2: K2, p to last 2 sts, k2.

Rep these 2 rows 8 times more (18 rows in total).

Break off yarn and leave sts on a spare needle.

Complete second side to match but do not break off yarn.

Next row: K30, then k2tog using last st from this needle and first st from spare needle, k across rem sts on spare needle (61 sts).

Purl 1 row.

Shape top

Next row: *(k8, skpo); rep from * to last st, k1.

Next and alt rows: P all sts.

Next row: *k7, skpo); rep from * to last st, k1.

Cont as set until the row '*(k1, skpo); rep from * to last st' has been worked.

Knit one row.

Cast off.

Making up

Join garter stitch lower border. Join handle side from the top down to just above where the 2-st g-st border begins, leaving a hole for the knob of the teapot. Sew in ends of yarn.

There's no right or wrong side to this cover by Frankie Brown – the textured stitch produces a reversible fabric with embossed diamonds on one side and cabled diamonds on the other.

Double diamonds

Materials
Sirdar Country Style DK (348yds/318m per 100g)
1 × 100g ball Dusty Pink 423
A pair of 3.25mm (US3:UK10) needles
A pair of 4mm (US6:UK8) needles

Special techniques
Inc: increase by working into the front, then the back of stitch
M1p: increase by purling into the front, then the back of the stitch
P2tog tbl: purl 2 sts together through the back of the loops
Diamond pattern (see instructions)

Tension
11 sts and 15 rows to 10cm over stocking stitch using 4mm needles

Sides (make 2)

Using 3.25mm needles and the long tail method cast on 41 sts and work 5 rows in k1, p1 rib.

Next row: *Rib 3, inc in next st; rep from * to last st, k1 (51 sts).

Change to 4mm needles and foll the 20-row diamond patt, noting that all incs are made purlwise (m1p).

Diamond pattern

Row 1: K8, (p3, k1, p3, k11) twice, p3, k4.

Row 2: K3, (p1, m1p, k3, p2tog, p7, p2tog tbl, k3, m1p) twice, p1, m1p, k3, p2tog, p3, K3.

Row 3: K7, (p3, k3, p3, k9) twice, p3, k5.

Row 4: K3, p2, (m1p, k3, p2tog, p5, p2tog tbl, k3, m1p, p3) twice, m1p, k3, p2tog, p2, k3.

Row 5: K6, (p3, k5, p3, k7) twice, p3, k6.

Row 6: K3, p3, (m1p, k3, p2tog, p3, p2tog tbl, k3, m1p, p5) twice, m1p, k3, p2tog, p1, k3.

Row 7: K5, (p3, k7, p3, k5) twice, p3, k7.

Row 8: K3, p4, (m1p, k3, p2tog, p1, p2tog tbl, k3, m1p, p7) twice, m1p, k3, p2tog, k3.

Row 9: K4, (p3, k9, p3, k3) twice, p3, k8.

Row 10: K3, p5, (m1p, k3, p3tog, k3, m1p, p9) twice, m1p, k3, p2tog, k2.

Row 11: K3, (p3, k11, p3, k1) twice, p3, k9.

Row 12: K3, p4, (p2tog tbl, k3, m1p, p1, m1p, k3, p2tog, p7) twice, p2togtbl, k3, m1p, k3.

Row 13: K4, (p3, k9, p3, k3) twice, p3, k8.

Row 14: K3, p3, (p2tog tbl, k3, m1p, p3, m1p, k3, p2tog, p5) twice, p2togtbl, k3, m1p, p1, k3.

Row 15: K5, (p3, k7, p3, k5) twice, p3, k7.

Row 16: K3, p2, (p2tog tbl, k3, m1p, p5, m1, k3, p2tog, p3) twice, p2togtbl, k3, m1p, p2, k3.

Row 17: K6, (p3, k5, p3, k7) twice, p3, k6.

Row 18: K3, p1, (p2tog tbl, k3, m1p, p7, m1p, k3, p2tog, p1) twice, p2togtbl, k3, m1p, p3, k3.

Row 19: K7, (p3, k3, p3, k9) twice, p3, k5.

Row 20: K3, p2tog tbl, (k3, m1p, p9, m1p, k3, p3tog) twice, k3, m1p, p4, k3.

Work 30 rows in this diamond patt. Change to 3.25mm needles and work 20 further rows in patt.

Decrease for top

Work in g-st throughout.

Next row: K1, *k2tog, rep from * to end (26 sts).

Knit 4 rows.

Next row: *k2tog, rep from * to end (13 sts).

Knit 4 rows.

Next row: *k1, k2tog, rep from * to end (9 sts).

Knit 3 rows.

Cast off loosely using a 4mm needle.

Making up

Join seam for 1¼in (3cm) at the lower edge and 2½in (6cm) at the top for the handle seam. Join 1in (2.5cm) at the lower edge and 4in (10cm) at the top for spout seam. These measurements are approximate: try the cozy on the pot and adjust as necessary before fastening off.

Tip

If you want this cozy to be reversible, take care to join the pattern pieces very neatly and sew in all the ends.

This mouthwatering trio by Nicola Haisley looks good enough to eat. It's the perfect complement for good old-fashioned tea and cakes.

Fondant fancy

Materials

Tawny Family Favourites Double Knitting (328yds/300m per 100g)
1 x 100g ball White 1 (M)
James C Brett Top Value Double Knitting
1 x 100g ball Lemon 8412, Pink 8421 or Brown 8410 (C)
Oddments of dark brown or white yarn for the stitched icing drizzle
A pair of 5.5mm (US9:UK5) needles

Tension

8 sts and 11 rows to 4in (10cm) over stocking stitch using 5.5mm needle and double yarn, unstretched

First side

Yarns are used double throughout.
Using M double, cast on 34 sts using the thumb method.
Work 20 rows in k1, p1 rib.
Break off yarn.
Change to C used double.
Next row: Knit 5, *(k2tog, k5); rep from * to last 8 sts, k2tog, k6 (30 sts).
Next row: Purl.
Beg knit, st st 6 rows.**
Break off yarn and leave sts on a holder.

Second side

Work as for first half to **.
Next row: With RS facing, knit across all sts from both halves (60 sts).
Next row: Purl.
Next row: K2, *(k2tog, k4); rep from * to last 4 sts, k2tog, k2 (50 sts).
Next row: Purl.
Next row: K2, *(k2tog, k3); rep from * to last 3 sts, k2tog, k1 (40 sts).
Next row: Purl.
Next row: K1, *(k2tog, k2); rep from * to last 3 sts, k2tog, k1 (30 sts).

Next row: Purl.
Next row: K2, *(k2tog, k1); rep from * to last 4 sts, k2tog, k2 (21 sts).
Next row: Purl.
Next row: (k2tog) five times, k1, (k2tog) five times (11 sts).
Cut yarn leaving a long tail and draw through sts, pulling tight.

Nobble

Using C double, cast on 20 sts.
Beg knit, st st 2 rows.
Next row: K2tog across row (10 sts).
Cut yarn leaving a long tail.
Draw yarn through sts and pull tight, then sew up seam.

Making up

Sew down top seam to match the other side. Join lower edge to allow room for handle and spout. Attach the nobble to top of cake. Using dark brown or white yarn, embroider the icing drizzle in chain stitch.

Tip

The cozy is shown in all three colour variations but you can choose your own. The 'nobble' can be made in red to look like a cherry if you prefer!

Whatever the weather, this cheerful design by Colleen Webster will hold the promise of a bright day. Use all the colours of the rainbow as shown, or just use up oddments.

Rainbow bright

Materials

Any DK yarn

Approx 25g in each of the following shades: red, orange, yellow, green, blue, dark blue and violet

1 × 50g ball DK yarn in a toning shade for lining

A pair of 4mm (US6:UK8) needles

A pair of 5mm (US8:UK6) needles

A pair of 7mm (US10.5:UK2) needles

Special techniques

Wyb: with yarn at back of work

Drop stitch pattern (see instructions)

Tension

Outer cozy: not critical as pattern is very stretchy

Lining: 14 sts measure 4in (10cm) in width over stocking stitch on 5mm needles, with yarn used double

Sides (make 2)

Note: yarns are used double throughout.
Using two strands of violet, cast on 33 sts and k 1 row.
Change to 7mm needles and work in patt, carrying yarns not in use up the side of the work, as folls:

Pattern

Row 1: Using violet, *(k3, wyb, sl1 p-wise); rep from * to end.
Row 2: K1, *(yf, sl1 p-wise, yb, k3); rep from * to end.
Row 3: Using red, k1, *(wyb, sl1 p-wise, k3); rep from * to end.
Row 4: *(k3, yf, sl1 p-wise, yb); rep from *to last st, k1.
These four rows form the pattern.
Rows 5 and 6: Using orange, rep rows 1 and 2.
Rows 7 and 8: Using yellow, rep rows 3 and 4.
Rows 9 and 10: Using green, rep rows 1 and 2.
Rows 11 and 12: Using blue, rep rows 3 and 4.
Rows 13 and 14: Using dark blue, rep rows 1 and 2.
Cont in patt until 38 rows in total have been worked, ending after a second row in green. Break off all yarn except green.
Next row (dec): *(k2, k2tog); rep from * to last st, k1 (25 sts).
Next row: P.

Next row: *(k2, k2tog); rep from * to last st, k1 (19 sts).
Next row: P.
Next row: *(k2, k2tog); rep from * to last 3 sts, k3 (15 sts).
Next row: P.
Next row: *(k2 tog); rep from * to last st, k1 (8 sts).
Work 6 rows in stocking stitch on these 8 sts for spike.
Next row: (k2tog) to end (4 sts).
Break off yarn leaving a long end. Thread through rem sts and fasten off.

Lining (make 2)

Using two strands of DK and 5mm needles, cast on 31 sts and work 20 rows in st st. Break off yarn and place sts on a holder.
Complete the second side to match but do not break off yarn.
Next row: K30, then k2tog using the last st from this needle and the first st from the spare needle, k across rem sts on spare needle (61 sts).
Purl one row.

Shape top

Next row: *(k8, skpo); rep from * to last st, k1.
Next and alternate rows: P all sts.
Next row: *k7, skpo); rep from * to last st, k1.
Cont in this way until the row *(k1, skpo); rep from * to last st has been worked.
Cast off very loosely.

Making up
Cozy

Join first 6 rows of the lower edge of outer cozy. Join the top spike, then join downwards for approx 4in (10cm) for the spout side.

Lining

Join the first 2 rows of lower edge. Join lining approx 4in (10cm) down from the top. Place inside outer cozy and join at handle and spout openings, making sure all ends of yarn carried up the side are hidden by the edge of the lining. Catch lining loosely in place all round lower edge of cozy.

Tiny buttons in the shape of bees inspired this design by Frankie Brown.
The cheerful sunflowers are worked separately and sewn on,
while the leaves are part of the cable pattern.

Sunflower garden

Materials

Sirdar Country Style DK (348yds/318m per 100g)

Approx 50g Green 419 (M)

Oddments of yellow and brown 4-ply yarn for sunflowers

A pair of 2.75mm (US2:UK12) needles

A pair of 3.25mm (US3:UK10) needles

A pair of 4mm (US6:UK8) needles

Cable needle

Assorted buttons to decorate

Special techniques

Inc 1: work into the front, then the back of the next st to inc

C6R: slip 3 sts on to a cable needle and hold at back, k3, then p3 from the cable needle

C6L: slip 3 sts on to a cable needle and hold at front, p3, then k3 from the cable needle

Sl1p-wise: slip 1 stitch with needles held as if to purl

Wyib: with the yarn in back

Tension

22 sts and 30 rows measure 4in (10cm) over stocking stitch on 4mm needles.

Sides (make 2)

Using 3.25mm needles, the long tail method and M, cast on 41 sts and work 9 rows k1, p1 rib.

Next row: *(p1, inc1); rep from * to last st, p1 (61 sts).

Change to 4mm needles and work the background for the sunflowers:

Leaf pattern background

Row 1: K3, p5, (k6, p7) three times; k6, p5, k3.

Row 2: K8, (p6, k7) three times; p6, k8.

Row 3: As row 1.

Row 4: As row 2.

Row 5: K3, p2, (C6R, C6L, p1) four times; p1, k3.

Row 6: K5, (p3, k6, p3, k1) four times; k4.

Row 7: K3, p2, (k3, p6, k3, p1) four times; p1, k3.

Row 8: As row 6.

Row 9: As row 7.

Row 10: As row 6.

Row 11: K3, p2, (k3tog, p6, k3tog, p1) four times, p1, k3 (45 sts).

These 11 rows complete the section. Work the next 7 rows in rev st st with a g-st border thus:

Wrong side rows: Knit.

Right side rows: K3, p to last 3 sts, k3.

Next row: K3, k2tog, k to last 5 sts, k2tog, k3 (43 sts).

Now work 5 rows in slip stitch rib thus:

Slip stitch rib

Row 1: K5, *(p3, k2); rep from * to last 3 sts, k3.

Row 2: K3, p2, *(k1, sl1 p-wise wyib, k1, p2); rep from * to last 3 sts, k3.

Change to 3.25mm needles and work another 10 rows slip stitch rib.

Work 8 rows in g-st.

Next row: *(k1, k2tog); rep from * to last st, k1 (29 sts).

Beg with a purl row, work 3 rows in stocking stitch.

Next row: *(k2tog, k1); rep from * to last 2 sts, K2tog (19 sts).

Beg with a purl row, work 3 rows in stocking stitch.

Knit 2 rows.

Next row: *(k1, k2tog); rep from * to last st, k1 (13 sts).

Knit 1 row.

Next row: *(k1, k2tog); rep from * to last st, k1 (9 sts).

Knit 1 row.

Cast off loosely using a 4mm needle.

Sunflowers (make 8)

Using yellow 4-ply yarn and 2.75mm needles cast on 5 sts.

Next step: *cast off 3sts, K1, turn, K2, cast on 3 sts.

Rep from * until you have knitted a strip of 15 petals.

Cast off, leaving a length of yarn to sew up with. Sew a running stitch along the straight edge of the strip, pull to gather and join the two ends of the strip to complete the petals.

Centre of sunflower

Using brown 4-ply, cast on 2 sts.

Work in garter stitch, inc1 at the start of each row until there are 8 sts on the needle. Knit 2 rows straight.

Next step: Still working in garter stitch, k2tog at the start of each row until there are 2 sts on the needle. K2tog and finish off, leaving a length of yarn to sew up with.

Sew a running stitch round the edge of the piece and pull tight to gather. Knot to the end of yarn at the cast-on edge, then attach the centre to the middle of the petals.

Making up

Join 1¼in (3cm) at the lower edge and 2½in (6cm) at the top for the handle seam. Join 1in (2.5cm at the bottom and 4in (10cm) at the top for the spout seam. These are approximate measurements; after joining it is best to try the cozy on the teapot and adjust seams as necessary before fastening off.

Using green yarn sew the sunflowers in place on the tea cozy. Finally, using green sewing thread, attach the buttons of your choice. I used a few ladybird buttons and a hedgehog button from my stash. The bee buttons are available from Craftime, *www.craftime.com*

Tip

It is easier to position the decorations if you place the cozy on the pot first.

The stitch used for this design by Paula Coyle produces a textured fabric that looks just like a plump blackberry, but you could substitute red yarn if you prefer raspberries.

Purple berry

Materials

Twilley's Freedom Spirit (120m per 50g)

2 × 50g balls in 518 purple mix (used double throughout)

A pair of 4.5mm (US7:UK7) needles

A pair of 5mm (US8:UK6) needles

Darning needle

Special techniques

Butterfly stitch pattern (see instructions)

Sl5wyif: slip 5 sts with yarn held in front of work

Skpo: slip 1 st, k1, pass slipped st over

Tension

16 sts and 18 rows to 4in (10cm) measured over stocking stitch on 5mm needles

Sides (make 2)

Using a strand of yarn from each ball, cast on 39 sts and work 4 rows g-st. Work in pattern for 40 rows (2 reps).

Join top

Row 1: K2, *(sl5wyif, skpo, k1, k2tog); rep from * to last 6 sts, sl5wyif, sl1, k1 from holder, psso, k1, cont across sts on holder, rep from * to last 7 sts, sl5wyif, k2 tog.

Row 2: Purl all sts (64 sts).

Rep last 2 rows once.

Row 5: Skpo, *(sl5wyif, sl1, k2tog, psso); rep from * to last 6 sts, sl5wyif, k1 (49 sts).

Row 6: Purl.

Row 7: K1, *(sl5wyif, k1) to end (49 sts).

Row 8: P3, *(insert RH needle up through loose strands at front of work and transfer them to LH needle, purl next st so they slip over the top and are held by it, p5); rep from * ending last rep p3.

Row 9: Purl.

Row 10: K1, *(skpo, k1, k2tog, k1) to end (33 sts).

Row 11: Purl

Row 12: *(k1, skpo) to end (22 sts).

Row 13: Purl.

Row 14: (k2tog) to end (11 sts).

Row 15: Purl.

Row 16: Inc in each st to end (22 sts).

Work 5 rows st st.

Cast off.

Making up

Sew in ends of yarn. Join from the bottom of the cozy (spout side) about ¾in (2cm). Join down from the top, letting the reverse stocking stitch roll over and leaving a gap of about 3in (7.5cm) for the spout.

Butterfly stitch pattern

Rows 1, 3, 5, 7 and 9 (RS): K2, *(sl5wyif, k5); rep from * to end, sl5wyif, k2.

Rows 2, 4, 6 and 8: K1, p to last st, p1.

Row 10 (RS): K1, p3, *(insert right needle up through the loose strands at the front of work and transfer them to the left needle, p the next st so the strands slip over the top and are held by it, p9); rep from * across row, ending last rep p4.

Rows 11, 13, 15, 17 and 19: K7, *(sl5wyif, k5); rep from *to last 2 sts, k2.

Rows 12, 14, 16 and 18: K1, p to last st, k1.

Row 20: K1, p8, *(insert right needle up through the loose strands at the front of work and transfer them to the left needle, p the next st so the strands slip over the top and are held by it, p9); rep from * ending last rep p8, k1. Break off yarn and place sts on a holder.

Work the second side to match but do not break off yarn.

Tip

Do not strand the yarn too loosely across the front of the work when slipping the 5 sts, or the fabric will not pull in when they are gathered together on the next row.

Cat lovers will adore this cheerful design by Sheila Woolrich.
She added the little mouse peering nervously from the top
after a suggestion by her husband!

Cat and mouse

Materials

1 x 50g ball of any white DK yarn

1 x 50g ball of Lister Regatta DK in 871 grey/white/silver twist
or any grey-mix DK

Oddment of black and fawn DK for cat and mouse

Oddments of green, yellow, pink, blue and brown DK for
leaves and flowers

A pair of 5mm (US8:UK6) needles

A pair of 4mm (US6:UK8) needles

A pair of 3.25mm (US3:UK10) needles

A 3.25mm (USD/3:UK10) crochet hook

Special techniques

Garter stitch

Tension

Not critical as fabric is very stretchy

Sides (make 2)

Using one strand of white and one strand of grey mix together, cast on 29 sts and work in pattern:

Row 1: K3, *(p1, k1,p1,k1, p1,k4); rep from * across row, ending last rep k3.

Row 1: P4, *(k1, p1, k1, p6); rep from * across row, ending last rep p4.

Work for 40 rows in total.

Shape top

Row 1: K3, *(k2tog, k2); rep from * to last 2 sts, k2tog (22 sts).

Rows 2 and 4: Purl.

Row 3: K2, *(k2tog, k1); rep from * to last 2 sts, k2tog (15 sts).

Row 5: K1, *(k2tog); rep from * to end (8 sts).

Break yarn and thread through rem sts. Fasten off.

Making up

Sew up 1¾in (2cm) from bottom. Leave opening for handle and spout. Sew rem seam to top.

Small leaves (make 3)

Using 4mm needles and a single strand of green, cast on 8sts.

Next row: K6, turn.

Next row: Sl1, k3, turn.

Next row: Sl1, k to end.

Cast off all sts.

Large leaves (make 7)

Using 4mm needles and a single strand of green, cast on 12 sts.

Next row: K10, turn.

Next row: Sl1, k7, turn.

Next row: Sl1, k3, turn.

Next row: Sl1, k to end.

Cast off all sts.

Large flower

Using a 3.25mm hook and pink, make 5ch and ss into first ch to form a ring.

Round 1: 4ch, (1tr, 1ch) 7 times into ring, ss into third of 4ch.

Round 2: Ss into first ch sp, *(3ch, 3tr, 3ch, ss into ch sp, ss into next ch); rep from * to end.

Fasten off.

Small flowers
(make 1 blue, 4 yellow)

Using 4mm needles, cast on 16 sts.

Next row: (p2tog) to end (8 sts).

Thread yarn through rem sts and fasten off.

Join seam and embroider contrast cross stitch in centre.

Flower stems

Using 3.25mm hook and green, make 15 ch and fasten off. Make another, 10ch long, and fasten off.

Cat

Using 4mm needles and a single strand of black, cast on 8 sts.

Row 1: Knit.

Row 2: Knit, inc 1 st at each end.

Row 3: Knit.

Rows 4 and 5: As last 2 rows (12 sts).

Work 10 rows g-st.

Next row: Dec 1 st at each end.

Work 3 rows g-st.

Next row: Dec 1 st at each end of row (8 sts).

Work 2 rows g-st.

Next row: (k2tog) to end (4 sts).

Next row: Inc in every st (8 sts).

Work 2 rows g-st.

Next row: Inc 1 st at each end of row (10 sts).

Work 6 rows g-st.

Dec 1 st at each end of foll 2 rows (6 sts).

Shape ears

Next row: K3, turn.

Knit 1 row.

Next row: K3tog.

Fasten off. Rejoin yarn and complete other ear to match.

Tail

Using black, cast on 16 sts.

Cast off.

Mouse

Using 4mm needles, cast on 6 sts.

Row 1: Inc in every st to end (12 sts).

Beg purl, work 7 rows st st.

Change to 3.25mm needles.

Shape head

Row 9: K2tog, k8, k2tog (10 sts).

Rows 10, 12 and 14: Purl.

Row 11: K2tog, k6, k2tog (8 sts).

Row 13: (k2tog, k1) twice, k2tog (5 sts).

Thread yarn through rem sts. Fasten off.

Making up

Sew in ends of yarn. Join cover 1¼in (3cm) up from lower edge and approx 5in (13cm) from top, fitting on pot to check before fastening off. Attach cat to cozy, curving tail as shown.

Assemble 7 large leaves, the large flower and the small blue flower and attach to top. Assemble 3 small leaves, the stems and 4 small flowers and attach as shown.

Sew seam of mouse and stuff. Crochet chain for mouse's tail and make loops for ears. Embroider eyes and nose. Attach to cozy.

Spoil yourself with this delicate cabled design by Patti di Cagli.
The luxurious alpaca and angora-mix yarn is gorgeous to look at, sumptuously
soft, and is perfectly complemented by the toning velvet ribbon.

Toast

Materials

UK Alpaca luxury knit DK
1 x 100g ball in 03 Fawn
A pair of 3.75mm (US5:UK9)
Cable needle
1yd (1m) narrow velvet ribbon

Special techniques

Cables
Eyelets (see pattern instructions)
Picot edging (see pattern instructions)

Sides (make 2)

Using 3.75mm needles cast on 72 sts. and knit 4 rows.

Cable pattern

Row 1: k1, *[k2, p2]; rep. from * to last 3 sts, k3.

Row 2: k1, P2 *[k2, p2]: rep. from * to last st, k1.

Row 3: (cable row): k3, *[p2, C6B]; rep. from * to last 5 sts, p2, k3.

Row 4: as Row 2.

Rows 5 & 7: as Row 1.

Rows 6 & 8: as Row 2.

These 8 rows form the patt. Rep until work measures 6in (15cm), ending with a cable row.

Note: if your teapot is taller or shorter than a standard model, adjust the length here by working more or fewer rows.

Shape top

First dec row: (WS) K1, p2, k2, p2tog, *[p2, p2 tog, k2, p2 tog]; rep from * to last 5 sts; k2, p2 tog, k1 (55 sts).

Second dec row: k2, *[p2tog, k4]; rep from * to last 5 sts, p2 tog, k3 (46 sts).

First eyelet row: (WS): K1, p2, *(yrn, p2tog, p3); rep from * to last 5 sts, p2tog, yrn, p2tog, k1.

Beg with a knit row, work 8 rows st st.

Picot edging

Next row (RS): K1, *(k2tog, yo); rep. from * to last st, k1.

Beg with a purl row, work 8 rows st st.

Second eyelet row (WS): K1, p2, *(yrn, p2tog, p3); rep from * to last 5 sts, p2tog, yrn, p2tog, k1.

Beg with a knit row, work 4 rows st st. Cast off.

Making up

Press the tops of both sides of the cozy from the eyelet rows up. With right sides together, join side seams from the top down to 1in (2.5cm) below the first eyelet row. With work still inside out, fold top section down along picot edging row, so the picot edge is at the top. Sew cast-off edges to the wrong side of work, then turn work to the right side. Thread ribbon through eyelets and draw up into a bow. Try cozy on the pot for size and measure seams below the handle and spout, then join from the wrong side.

Tip

When attaching the edgings, place a spare needle through both sets of eyelets. This will keep them aligned and hold the work flat, making it easier to thread the ribbon through later.

Simple Fairisle spots decorate this design by Lucy Norris.
If you do not feel confident enough to work from a chart,
the instructions are also written out in full.

Black spotty

Materials

Rowan Handknit DK cotton (92yds/85metres per 50g ball)

1 x 50g ball 252 Black (M)

1 x 50g ball hot pink 313 Slick (A)

1 x 50g ball pale pink 310 Shell (B)

1 x 50g ball turquoise 318 Seafarer (C)

A pair of 4.5mm (US0:UK0) needles

Special techniques

Garter stitch

Fairisle

Tension

19 sts to 4in (10cm) in width over stocking stitch on
4.5mm needles

Sides (make 2)

Using M, cast on 82 sts and work 10 rows in g-st. Now work as folls:

Row 1: K41, turn and leave rem sts on holder.

Row 2: K2, p to last 2 sts, k2.

Row 3: K3M *(k2A, k6M); rep from * 4 times, k2A, k4M.

Row 4: K2M, p1M *(p4A, p4M); rep from * 4 times, k2M.

Row 5: K3M, *(k4A, k4M); rep from * 4 times, k2M.

Row 6: K2M, p1M *(p2A, p6M); rep from * 4 times, p2A, p2M, k2M.

Row 7: Knit, using M.

Row 8: K2, p to last 2 sts, k2 using M.

Rows 9–12: Work a set of spots in B, spacing each mid-way between two spots of the previous row.

Rows 13 and 14: As rows 7 and 8.

Rows 15–18: As rows 3–6 but working spots in C.

Rows 17–18: As rows 7 and 8. Work another set of spots in A, then another set of spots in B, spacing as before.

Next row: As row 7.

Break yarn and leave sts on a holder. Work second side to match.

Joining the sides

Next row: P41, p across sts from first side (82 sts).

Next 4 rows: Work a further set of spots using C.

Cont using M only.

Next row: K1, *(k6, k2 tog); rep from * to last st, k1.

Next row: P to end.

Next row: K1, *(k5, k2tog); rep from * to last st, k1.

Next row: P to end.

Next row: K1, *(k4, k2tog); rep from * to last st, k1.

Next row: P1, *(p2tog, p3); rep from * to last st, k1.

Next row: K1, *(k2, k2tog); rep from * to last st, K1.

Next row: P1, *(p2tog, p1); rep from * to end, p1.

Next row: K1, *(k1, k2tog); rep from * to end.

Next row: P1, (p2tog) to end, p1.

Break off yarn, thread through rem sts and pull tight.

Bobble

Using B, cast on 3 sts.

Row 1: Inc in first st, k1, inc in last st (5 sts).

Row 2: P2 into first st, p1, p2 into next st, p1, p2 into next st (8 sts).

Work 8 rows in stocking stitch.

Next row: K2tog, k1, k2tog, k1, k2tog (5 sts).

Next row: P2tog, p1, p2tog (3 sts).

Cast off.

Tie knot through last st and use running stitch to go round edge of knitted circle. Pull tight to form bobble.

Making up

Join side of cozy using mattress stitch to match other side. Attach bobble to top of cozy.

Black spotty chart *8 sts x 36 rows*

Each square = I st and I row

Read RS rows from R to L and WS rows from L to R

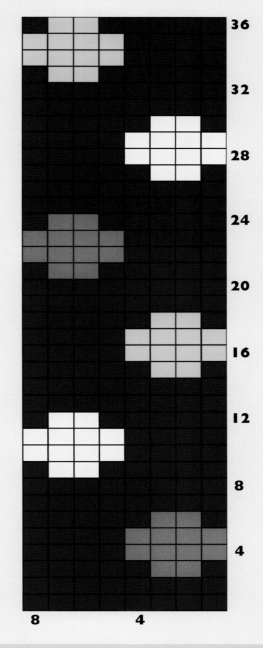

Turquoise (C)

Hot pink (A)

Pale pink (B)

Black (M)

This textured wool-mix cozy by Vikki Harding will cover your pot in restrained charm, and the shaggy pompon and pretty buttons add a funky touch.

Peru

Materials

Sirdar Peru Naturals (98yds/90m per 50g)

1 x 50g skein 0555 Pico (M)

1 x 50g skein 0550 Andean White (C)

A pair of 6mm (US10:UK4) bamboo needles

5mm crochet hook

3 x buttons

Special techniques

Making a pompon

Sl1p: slip 1 st purlwise (with yarn in front of work)

Tension

18 sts x 36 rows to 4in (10cm) over patt using 6mm needles (yarns used double throughout)

Note: yarns are used double throughout. You may find it easier to divide each ball into two smaller balls before you start, then wind the strands together on one ball before you begin to knit.

Sides (make 2)

Using two strands of M, cast on 38 sts and work in patt thus:

Pattern

Row 1: Using M, *(k1, sl1p), rep from * to end.
Row 2: Using C, *(sl1p, k1), rep from * to end.
Row 3: Using C, *(sl1, k1); rep from * to end.
Row 4: Using M, *(k1, sl1); rep from * to end.
These four rows form the pattern.
Rep patt for a further 32 rows.

Decrease for top

Row 37: Ssk, *(k1, sl1); rep from * to last 2 sts, k2tog (36 sts).
Row 38: Ssk, k1, * (sl1, k1); rep from * to last 3 sts, sl1, k2tog (34 sts).
Row 39: Ssk, *(sl1, k1); rep from * to last 2 sts, k2tog (32 sts).
Row 40: Ssk, sl1, *(k1, sl1); rep from * to last 3 sts, k1. K2tog (30 sts).
Rows 41–49 inclusive: Cont in patt with no decs.
Row 50: Ssk, *(sl1, k1); rep from * to last 2 sts, k2tog.

Row 51: Ssk, k1, *(sl1, k1); rep from * to last 3 sts, sl1, k2tog (26 sts).
Row 52: Ssk, *(k1, sl1); rep from * to last 2 sts, k2tog (24 sts).
Row 53: Ssk, sl1, *(k1, sl1); rep from * to last 3 sts, sl1, k2tog (22 sts).
Row 54: Ssk, *(sl1, k1); rep from * to last 2 sts, k2tog (20 sts).
Row 55: Ssk, k1, *(sl1, k1); rep from * to last 3 sts, sl1, k2tog (18 sts).
Row 56: Ssk. *(k1, sl1); rep from * to last 2 sts, k2tog (16 sts).
Row 57: Ssk, sl1, *(k1, sl1); rep from * to last 3 sts, k1, k2tog (14 sts).
Row 58: Ssk, *(sl1, k1); rep from * to last 2 sts, k2tog (12 sts).
Row 59: K1, *(sl1, k1); rep from * to last st, sl1.
Row 60: Sl1, *(k1, sl1) to last st, k1.
Row 61: Sl1, *(k1, sl1); rep from * to last st, k1.
Row 62: K1, *(sl1, k1); rep from * to last st, sl1.
Row 63: K1, *(sl1, k1); rep from * to last st, k1.
Cast off using M.

Making up

Join sides on the spout edge, leaving a gap for the spout. Join all the way to the top, across the cast-off edges and about ⅜in (1cm) down handle side.

Crocheted border

Beg at lower edge on one side, work a dc border round handle side to neaten edges, dec by working 3 sts tog at the top to stop it splaying out. Make 14-ch button loops above the handle, in the centre of the handle and at the lower edge. After each chain loop, work 1 dc back into the same st and cont in dc. Work dc round spout side, dec at top and lower edge as before.

Attach buttons. Sew in yarn ends. Make a fairly loose pompon using both yarns and attach to top of cozy.

Yummy pastels make this design by Alexandra McKee a feast for the eyes. The technique used to increase stitches may seem complicated at first, but will soon become clear.

Cupcake

Materials

King Cole Smooth DK (236yds/216metres per 100g)

1 x 100g ball in Yellow 880 (A)

1 x 100g ball in Blue 856 (B)

Sirdar Snuggly Tiny Tots (150yds/137 metres per 50g)

1 x 50g ball in 0975 Sweetheart

Oddment of green yarn for leaves

A pair of 4mm (US6:UK8) needles

A 4mm (US6:UK8) circular needle

4 x 4mm (US6:UK8) double-pointed needles

3 x decorative clear buttons

Special techniques

Making a pompon

Inc1p: increase 1 stitch purlwise

Inc1k: increase 1 stitch knitwise

Tension

31 sts and 30 rows to 4in (10cm) over 2-colour k2, p2 rib using 4mm needles, unstretched

Note: make each inc between 2 sts of the same colour and type on the previous row: when working between 2 sts in A, inc using B; when working bet 2 sts in B, inc using A. Work incs between p sts k-wise; work incs between k sts p-wise.

Side 1

Using 4mm needles and yarn A, cast on 50 sts and work in patt for base:

Row 1: *(k2A, p2B), rep from * to end of row.

Rows 2–6: Rib as set, keeping all yarn crossovers to WS of work.

Row 7: Dec1, rib 11, inc1p, rib 25, inc1k, rib to end.

Row 8 and 9: Work in rib, dec 1 st at each end of row.

Row 10: Work in rib as set.

Row 11: Rib 10, inc1p, rib 27, inc1k, rib to end.

Row 15: Rib 9, inc1k, rib 28, inc1p, rib to end.

Row 19: Rib 13, inc1k, rib 29, inc1p. Work 7 rows rib as set.

Row 27: Inc1 at each end, working extra sts into rib patt.

Next 2 rows: as row 27. Work 1 row, ending on a WS row. Place sts on a holder.

Side 2

Work as for side 1, but reversing order of rib and colour order. Take care to reverse all colour changes to suit incs indicated, for example:

Row 1: *(p2B, k2A); rep from * to end of row.

Top

RS facing, place completed sides on a circular needle, and place marker at beg of sts (116 sts).

Using C, work in the round for 4 rows. Transfer sts evenly across 3 double-pointed needles, then work as folls:

Row 5: *(k11, k2tog); rep from * 7 times, k10, k2tog.

Row 6: *(k9, k2T); rep from * 7 times, k8, k2T.

Row 7: *(k8, k2tog); rep from * 7 times, k7, k2tog.

Row 8: *(k7, k2tog); rep from * 7 times, K6, k2tog.

Row 9: *(k6, k2tog); rep from * 7 times, K5, k2tog.

Row 10: *(k5, k2tog); rep from * 7 times, K4, k2tog.

Row 11: *(k4, k2tog); rep from * 7 times, K3, k2tog.

Row 12: *(k3, k2tog); rep from * 7 times, K2, k2tog.

Row 13: *(k2, k2tog); rep from * 7 times, K1, k2tog.

Row 14: *(k1, k2tog); rep from * 7 times, K2.

Row 15: (k2tog) 9 times.

Row 16: (k2tog) 4 times, k1.

Row 17: (k2tog) twice, k1.

Cut yarn leaving a tail long enough to thread through rem 3 sts twice. Pull up tightly to close hole. Thread through centre of top to WS and secure.

Leaves (make 3)

Cast on 5 sts

Row 1 (RS): K2, yo, k2 (7 sts).

Row 2 and all even-numbered rows: Purl.

Row 3: K3, yo, k1, yo, k3 (9 sts).

Row 5: Ssk, k5, k2tog (7 sts).

Row 7: Ssk, k3, k2tog (5 sts).

Row 9: Ssk, k1, k2tog (3 sts).

Row 11: Sl1, k2tog, psso (1 st). Fasten off.

Making up

Join the sides at the top and base, leaving decreased edges free for spout and handle. Decorate the top of the cupcake with the leaves, a small pink pompon and buttons as shown.

This design by Emma Rennie is perfect if your teapot is not a standard shape – it just drops over the whole pot. It's felted for thickness and warmth, and the sewn-on yarn plait and star cut from knitted fabric add interest.

Felted

Materials

Anchor Wash + Filz-It (55yds/50m per 50g)
4 x 50g balls Pink 00011 (M)
1 x 50g ball Rose 00010 (C)
Oddment of Sirdar Freedom Wool DK in variegated green
A pair of 7mm (US10.5:UK2) needles
Large, sharp needle for blanket stitch
Sewing needles and rose-pink thread
Fabric 10 x 27in (25 x 74cm) approx for lining (optional)

Special techniques

Garter stitch
Skpo: slip 1 st, k1 st, pass slipped st over knitted st to dec
Felting (see instructions)

Measurements

Approx 9½in high x 13in wide after felting (24 x 33cm)

Sides (make 2)

Using M, cast on 50 sts and work 2 rows in g-st.

Join in C and work 2 rows in g-st.

Using M, work a further 4 rows in g-st. Cont in stocking stitch without shaping until piece measures about 8in (20cm). *Note: adjust height here if necessary, remembering that work will shrink by approx 30% during felting process.*

Shape top

Next row: Skpo, k to end, k2tog.
Next row: P all sts.
Rep last 2 rows 4 times more (40 sts).
Cont in stocking stitch, dec 1 st at each end of every row until there are 34 sts on the needle, ending on a WS row.
Next: Join in C and work 2 rows in g-st, cont to dec on every row.
Work 2 rows in stocking stitch, dec as before.
Cast off.

Fabric for appliqué

Using 5mm needles and Freedom DK, cast on 30 sts and work 40 rows in stocking stitch. Cast off.

Felting

Sew in yarn ends. Place each side of cozy in a separate nylon mesh bag or pillowcase, and knitted green square in a separate bag. Place in drum of washing machine with a bath towel or a pair of jeans to provide the friction necessary for felting. Add a small amount of washing powder and run through a full cycle at 40°C.

Remove the pieces and check that they have felted sufficiently. Pull gently to shape: each finished side of the cozy should measure approximately 13½in (14cm) wide and 8½in (22cm) high. Pull the green square to shape. Allow to dry completely. Press all pieces.

Edging

Cut lengths of pink Wash + Filz-It and green Freedom Wool about 1yd (1m) long and bind one end securely. Make a thick plait using the entire length of the yarn. Bind the other end.

Star

Cut out a star shape from the green square of knitted, felted fabric using the template provided. Place on one side of the cozy and pin in position. Using one strand of matching yarn. blanket-stitch in place.

Making up

Place sides of the cozy wrong sides together, and pin. Using matching sewing thread, oversew seams. Pin yarn plait in place over seam, tucking bound ends under, and sew in place.

Lining (optional)

If you wish to line your cozy, cut two pieces of coordinating cotton fabric using the sides as a guide. Add seam and hem turnings. Join the pieces, snipping into the curves, then press seam open. Insert in cozy, wrong sides together, and matching up seams. Turn in the hem edge to the wrong side and catch stitch to the lower edge of the cozy.

Tip

If using a pillowcase for felting, pin the flap so the piece does not escape during the washing process.

Star template (actual size)

This gorgeous design by Patti di Cagli will bring back the memory of lazy summer cream teas, even if you're just grabbing a quick cuppa and a biscuit in the depths of winter.

Strawberries & cream

Materials

Blue Sky organic cotton (150yds/137m per 50g)

1 x 100g ball in shade 80 (cream)

Rowan DK cotton (92yds/85m per 50g)

A small amount of 215 red

A small amount in 090 green

A pair of 4.5mm needles (UK7:US7)

1 pair 3.35mm needles (UK10:US3)

Small quantity of stuffing (kapok or an old pair of tights)

Special techniques

Make bobble (MB): [p1, k1 twice], p1) into same st (5 sts); pass 2nd, 3rd, 4th and 5th sts, one at a time, over first st on the RH needle.

Tension

Not crucial as fabric is very stretchy

Body (make 2 alike)

Using 4.5mm needles cast on 43 sts and work in pattern.

Bobble rib pattern

Rows 1 and 5 (RS): *P1, k1; rep from * to last st, p1.

Rows 2, 4, 6 and 8 (WS): *K1, p1; rep from * to last st., k1.

Row 3 (bobble row): *P1, k1, MB; rep from * to last st, k1.

Row 7 (2nd bobble row): *P1, MB, p1, k1; rep from * to end.

These 8 rows form the patt.

Rep rows 1–8 once.

Now work in p1, k1 rib until work measures 6in (15cm) from cast-on row, ending with a WS row.

Note: adjust height here if necessary to suit the height of your teapot.

Shape top

Row 1 (RS): P1, *skpo, p2tog; rep from * to last 2 sts, k2tog (22 sts).

Next row (WS): *P1, k1; rep from * to end.

Next row: *P1, skpo; p2tog; rep from * to last st, k1 (12 sts).

Next row: *P1, k1; rep from * to end.

Next row: (K2tog) 6 times.

Leave rem 6 sts on a stitch holder or spare needle, leaving a tail about 8in (20cm) long.

Complete second side to match the first, leaving final 6 sts on the needle.

Joining the sides

Working in k1, p1 rib, work across 6 sts left from second side, then pick up and work across 6 sts from holder, joining tail ends of yarn with a knot in centre of row (12 sts).

Work across these sts in k1, p1 rib for a further 7 rows.

Cast off in rib.

Strawberries (make 3)

Using 3.25mm (UK10:US3) needles and red, cast on 10 sts.

Row 1: Knit.

Row 2: Purl.

Row 3: *K1, (p1, k1) into next st; rep from * to end (15 sts).

Row 4: Purl.

Row 5: *K1, (p1, k1) into next st; rep from * to last st, k1 (22 sts).

Row 6: Purl.

Row 7: *K3 red, k1 green; (k4 red, k1 green) 3 times, twisting yarns tog between cols to avoid holes, rep from * to last 3 sts, k3 red.

Row 8: *P2 red, p3 green; rep from * to last 2 sts, p2 red. Cut red yarn, leaving a tail about 8in (20cm) long.

Row 9: Using green, knit all sts.

Row 10: (P2tog) 11 times, p1.

Row 11: (K2tog) 6 times.

Row 12: (P2tog) 3 times (11 sts).

Work 4 rows in stocking stitch over rem 3 sts. Cast off, leaving a tail about 8in (20cm) long.

Making up

Fold strawberry in half with right sides out. Using the green tail, join along stem edge and green part from the outside. Join the red part of the berry to about halfway, using the red tail. Fill with stuffing, then complete the seam and fasten off, pulling the strawberry to a point as you work. Fold cozy in half, right sides facing. Use long ends to join across top of cast-off edge and side seams, leaving room for the spout and handle. Sew in ends.

An easy loop stitch pattern gives this design by Susan Fortune excellent insulating properties, while the plush chenille yarn lends it an old-fashioned feel.

Chenille chic

Materials
Texere Plush Chenille (131yds/120m per 100g ball)
2 x 100g balls Merlot
A pair of 4mm (US6:UK8) needles
1½yds (1.5m) narrow organza ribbon
Needle and matching thread

Special techniques
Garter stitch (g-st)
Loop stitch: see instructions

Tension
17 sts measure approx 4in (10cm) over loop stitch patt on 4mm needles

Sides (make 2)

Using a cable cast-on and two strands of yarn tog, cast on 35 sts. Work 6 rows in g-st for a firm base.

Loop stitch pattern

Row 1: *(k1 but do not remove st from needle; yf, take yarn clockwise round thumb to form a loop; yb; holding loop in place with thumb; knit into st again [2 sts on needle]; pass first st over second to secure loop). Rep from * to end (35 sts).
Row 2: Knit.
These 2 rows form patt. Rep until work measures 4in (20cm) ending with a RS row.
Next row: (p5, p2tog) to end of row (30 sts).
Work in patt until work measures approx 5in (13cm) ending on RS.
Next row: (p4, p2tog) to end of row (25 sts).
Work 2 more rows in patt, ending on a RS row.
Next row: (p3, p2tog) to end of row (20 sts).
Work 2 more rows in patt, ending with a RS row.
Next row: (p2tog) to end of row (10 sts).*
Next row: (p2tog) to end (5 sts).
Knit 1 more row.
Cast off.
Make another piece the same.

Variation

If you would prefer a plainer cozy without a tassel and bow, cast off at * when 10 sts rem. Join sides, leaving gaps for handle and spout. There will be a circular opening at the top edge to accommodate the knob of the teapot.

Loopy tassel

Wind spare yarn round a piece of card approx 4in (10cm) wide. Slide loops of yarn from card and tie firmly in the centre, leaving a long end. Do not cut loops. Sew a few stitches through tied centre to secure. Fluff out loops.

Making up

Join sides of cozy on the WS using matching sewing thread, leaving gaps for handle and spout. Using a running stitch, gather the stitches at the top of the cozy to close the gap and form a base for the tassel. Attach tassel firmly to centre top. Cut organza ribbon into two equal lengths and tie between cozy and tassel, forming a double bow.

This cheeky elephant design makes an ideal teacozy – the spout forms a perfect trunk! Charmaine Fletcher added a touch of bling with a beaded, gold-trimmed headdress and bell-shaped tassels.

Assam

Materials

Sirdar Balmoral (125m per 50g ball)

2 x 50g balls 0474 grey

Twilley's Goldfingering (218m/200yds per 50g ball)

1 x 25g ball WG2 gold

Small quantities of red and cream yarn for headdress and tusks; oddment of black for eyes; gold embroidery thread

A pair each of 4mm (US6:UK8), 3.75mm (US5:UK9) and 3mm (US2/3:UK11) needles

A set of 3.25mm (US3:UK10) double-pointed needles

A small crochet hook (1.1mm or similar)

Darning, beading and sewing needles

Special techniques

Moss stitch

Making an I-cord

Mattress stitch

Tension

17 sts and 37 rows to 4in (10cm) over moss stitch on 4mm needles

Measurements

19in (48cm) maximum width excluding handle and spout

Note: the sides are worked from bottom to top and joined. The ears are worked as left- and right-facing pieces resembling a square with the corner missing, and sewn into shape before attaching to the cozy. An I-cord gathers the top.

Sides (make 2)

Using 4mm needles, cast on 40 sts using the thumb method.
Work in moss stitch pattern:

Moss stitch pattern

Row 1: P1, k1 to end.
Row 2: K1, p1 to end.
These two rows form patt. Rep until work measures 7¼in (18.5cm).

Eyelet section

Row 1: Knit to end.
Row 2: Purl to end.
Row 3: (eyelets): K4, *(yrn, k2tog, k2); rep from * to last 4 sts, yrn, k4.
Row 4: Purl to end
Row 6: Knit to end.
Cont in moss st patt for a further 1⅓in (3cm), ending with a RS row. At this point the side should measure 9in (23cm). Cast off, leaving a long tail.
Make another piece the same.

Left-facing ear

*Using 4mm needles and grey, cast on 25 sts and work in m-st patt for 2⅓in (6cm), ending on a WS row.
Now begin to dec on RS of work only, keeping decs in patt by knitting or purling sts tog as appropriate.*
Next row 1 (dec): M-st 23, work 2 sts tog (24 sts).
Next and every alt row: Work in m-st without dec.
Next row (dec): M-st 22, dec over last 2 sts (23 sts).
Cont in this way until 14 sts rem, ending on a RS row.
Cast off, leaving a long end.

Right-facing ear

Work as for left-facing ear from * to *.
Next row: Work 2 sts tog, m-st 23 (24 sts).
Next row: Work in m-st without dec.
Cont thus, dec 1 st at beg of each RS row until 14 sts rem, ending on a RS row.
Cast off, leaving a long end.

Tusks (make 2)

Using 3.75mm needles and cream, cast on 4 sts and work 4 rows st st.
Row 5: Knit, inc 1 st each end (6 sts).
Row 6 and every alt row: Purl.
Row 7: Knit.
Row 9: As row 5 (8 sts).
Row 11: Knit.
Row 13: As row 5 (10 sts).
Row 15: Knit.
Row 17: As row 5 (12 sts).
Row 19: As row 5 (14 sts).
Cast off k-wise, leaving a long tail. The tusk should measure approx 3in (7.5cm) and will curl naturally when sewn up.

Main headdress

Using 3.75mm needles and red yarn, cast on 7 sts.
Row 1 and every alt row: Knit.
Row 2: K1, m1, k6 (8 sts).
Row 4: K1, m1, k7 (9 sts).
Row 6: K1, m1, k8 (10 sts).
Row 8: K1, m1, k9 (11 sts).
Row 10: K1, m1, k10 (12 sts).
Row 12: K1, m1, k11 (13 sts).
Row 14: K1, m1, k12 (14 sts).
Row 16 (dec): K1, k2tog, k to end of row (13 sts).
Cont to dec thus on every alt row until 7 sts rem.
Cast off.

Central panel

Using 3mm needles and Goldfingering, cast on 3 sts. Beg k1, p1, k1, work in moss-st until the panel measures approx 7in (7.5cm). Cast off.

Assembling the headdress

Beg the patt again from row 2 and work to row 16. Rep until there are 16 scallops in total. Cast off.

Cont to inc on every alt row until there are 6 sts.

Row 1 and every alt row: Knit.
Row 10: K1, k2tog, k3 (5 sts).
Row 12: K1, k2tog, k2 (4 sts).
Row 14: K1, k2tog, k1 (3 sts).
Row 15: K1, k2tog (2 sts).
Row 16: K2.
Row 2: K1, m1, k1 (3 sts).
Rows 9, 11 and 13: Knit.

Scalloped border

Sew beads and sequins to the narrow central panel using invisible thread and placing approx ½in (1cm) apart. Leave the top sequin until later, as it will help to conceal the join between the panel and the braid. Position gold braid round the red cap, cast-off edge uppermost. The central point should be flanked by two braid points to which securing loops will be attached. There should be a braid point on either side of the pointed section of the red cap. Pin braid in place, then sew using gold embroidery thread. Pin and stitch central panel in place and position final sequin on join. Thread six gold beads and a drop on invisible thread and attach to centre front of headdress. Using 3mm needles and Goldfingering, cast on 2 sts, leaving a long tail. Work the first scallop thus:

Securing loops (make 2)

With the assembled headdress RS facing, work a loop into the RH of the 3 scallops at the top edge thus:
Insert a 1.1mm crochet hook into the central point of the scallop. Make 10ch, 1ss into central point to form a loop. Work 16dc around loop to form a teardrop shape. Fasten off.
Make second loop in the LH scallop at the top edge.

I-cord

Using two 3.25mm double-pointed needles, cast on 3 sts and work in I-cord for approx 24in (60cm). Cast off.

Bells (make 2)

Using 4mm needles and red, cast on 15 sts leaving a long tail.
Rows 1–4: Purl.
Beg knit, work in st st until work measures approx 1¼in (3cm) ending on a WS row. Do not cast off. Cut yarn leaving a tail of approx 8in (20cm). Thread tail on needle. Draw yarn in a circle; ease each st on to it but do not gather yet. Secure a strand of Goldfingering to cast-on edge and bind around the first st. Using backstitch, bind Goldfingering around each cast-on st to end to make a decorative pattern. Bind around the last st (17 gold sts in total). Using the cast-on tail, join the back seam to form the bell shape.

Eyes

Using 3mm needles and black, cast on 12 sts. Knit 1 row but do not cast off; break yarn leaving a long end and thread on to a darning needle. Pass yarn through each st in turn and join in a ring, joining cast-on edges tog to form a circle. Leave yarn end for attaching eyes.

Making up

Sides

Join the sides of the cozy from the lower edge, leaving gaps for handle and spout, then join upper seams, leaving a gap in central back seam to form an extra eyelet. Thread the I-cord through eyelets, beginning and ending at handle seam, and catching the securing loops from the headdress in the appropriate position. Tie a knot in each end of the I-cord, then ease the ring of cast-off sts at the top of a bell over each knot. Draw up the sts and sew in place, covering the knot. Place the cozy on the teapot ready to pin the ears, tusks, and eyes in place.

Ears

Using grey yarn, gather along the decreased incline (the short diagonal) using running stitches. Fasten off securely. Make two folds on either side of the centre of the gathered edge, creating an upside-down 'V'-shape, and stitch to secure. This provides the characteristic floppy shape. Run yarn back to end and use to attach ear to the head. Position the ears approx 3in (8cm) down from gathers and 4¼in (11cm) from spout gap edge. Sew in place using small stitches.

Tusks

Thread the cast-on tail on to a darning needle and draw the narrow ends in a circle. Close seam using mattress stitch. Place tusks approx 2⅓in (6cm) apart and 1⅓in (3.5cm) from the edge of the cozy, slanting outwards slightly. Sew in place.

Eyes

Attach eyes to front of the cozy, approx 5in (12.5cm) apart. Using the tail end, overstitch or blanket stitch around the outer edge. Fasten off.

Tip

When washing the cozy, it is best to remove the headdress and launder separately, reshaping while drying flat.

The bees that cluster over this ingenious design by Gina Woodward are placed randomly so add as many as you like, from a gentle hum to a swarm. It's an absolute honey of an addition to the tea table!

Beehive & blossom

Materials

Rowan Pure Wool DK (137 yds/125m per 50g ball)
1 x 50g ball main colour (M)
Rowan Pure Wool 4-ply (160m/174yds per 50g ball)
1 x 50g ball black
1 x 50g ball gold
A pair of 3.75mm (US5:UK9) needles
A pair of 3mm (US2/3:UK11) needles
A 2mm crochet hook

Tension

22 sts and 28 rows to 4in (10cm) over stocking stitch on 3.75mm needles

Note: the cozy is worked in a woven pattern with bees placed at random on RS rows, always into a knit stitch.

Sides (make 2)

Using 3.75mm needles and M, cast on 48 sts and work in beehive pattern:

Beehive pattern

Row 1 (RS): P5, *(k2, p4); rep from * to last st, p1.

Row 2: K5, *(p2, k4); rep from * to last st, k1.

Row 3: P5, *(k2, p4); rep from * to last st, p1.

Row 4: Purl.

Row 5: P2, (*k2, p4); rep from * to last 4 sts, k2, p2.

Row 6: K2, *(p2, k4); rep from * to last 4 sts, p2, k2.

Row 7: As row 5.

Row 8: Purl.

These 8 rows form the patt. Rep patt once more (16 rows in total).

Still working in patt, begin to place bees at random, always into a knit st.

Work until 36 rows of patt have been completed.

Shape top

Row 1: P2, k2, p4; *(k2, skpo, k2tog, k2)*; (p4, k2) twice; p4; work from * to * once more, p4, k2, p2 (44 sts).

Rows 2, 6, 10, 14 and 18: Knit all k sts; purl all p sts.

Row 3: P2, k2, p4; *(k1, skpo, k2tog, k1)*; (p4, k2) twice; p4; work from * to * once more; p4, k2, p2 (40 sts).

Rows 4, 8, 12, 16 and 20: Purl.

Row 5: P5, k2, p1; *(skpo, k2tog)*; p1; (k2, p4) twice; k2, p1; rep from * to * again; p1, k2, p5 (36 sts).

Row 7: P5, k2; *(skpo, k2tog)*; (k2, p4) twice; k2; work from * to * again; k2, p5 (32 sts).

Row 9: P2, k2, p2; *(skpo, k2tog)*; p2, k2, p4, k2, p2, work from * to * again; p2, k2, p2 (28 sts).

Row 11: P2, k2, p1; *(skpo, k2tog)*; p1, k2, p4, k2, p1, work from * to * again; p1, k2, p2 (24 sts).

Row 13: P4, *(skpo, k2tog)*; p3, k2, p3, work from * to * again; p4 (20 sts).

Row 15: P3, *(skpo, k2tog)*; p2, k2, p2, work from * to * again; p3 (16 sts).

Row 17: P2, *(skpo, k2tog)*; p4, work from * to * again; p2 (12 sts).

Row 19: P1, *(skpo, k2tog)*; p2, work from * to * again; p1 (8 sts).

Break off yarn and work second piece to match but do not break off sts.

Join top

Work across both pieces as folls:

Row 1 (RS): (P2tog) 8 times.

Row 2 (WS): K8.

Row 3: P8.

Cast off.

Bees

Row 1: Using black 4-ply, k1, yf, k1, yf, k1 into chosen stitch, turn.

Row 2: Purl all sts. 5 sts.

Rows 3–4: Using gold, work 2 rows in st st.

Work a further 6 rows in st st, alternating black and gold every 2 rows.

Row 11: Slip first 4 black sts over 5th st, then k 5th st using M.

Break off yarn, leaving approx 20in (52cm) of gold for wings.

Wings

Using a darning needle, bring end of gold yarn through to RS at edge of a gold stripe. Using 2mm crochet hook make 5ch, then work 4ss into first 4ch. Pull yarn through rem st, thread end through darning needle and take to WS of work. Bring yarn up on opposite side of stripe and make a second wing in the same way. Fasten off.

Blossom

Large outer petals
(make 7 pink and 7 white)

Using 3mm needles, cast on 42 sts and work 3 rows st st.

Row 4: (P3tog) across row (14 sts).

Row 5: (Skpo) across row (7 sts).

Break off yarn leaving an end of approx 19in (50cm). Thread through rem sts, draw up tightly and join side seam.

Smaller inner petals
(make 7 pink and 7 white)

Using 3mm needles cast on 24 sts and knit 1 row.

Row 2: (P3tog) across row (8 sts).

Row 3: (Skpo) across row (4 sts).

Break off yarn leaving an end of approx 4in (10cm). Thread through rem 4 sts, draw up tightly and join side seams.

Leaves (make 4)

Using 3mm needles and green, cast on 1 st.

Row 1: K1, yf, k1 into same st (3 sts).

Row 2 and every alt row: Purl.

Row 3: K1, yf, k1, yf, k1 (5 sts).

Row 5: K2, yf, k1, yf, k2 (7 sts).

Row 7: K3, yf, k1, yf, k4 (9 sts).

Row 9: k4, yf, k1, yf, k4 (11 sts).

Row 11: K4, k3tog, k4 (9 sts).

Row 13: K3, k3tog, k3 (7 sts).

Row 15: K2, k3tog, k2 (5 sts).

Row 17: K1, k3tog, k1; slip first 2 sts over third st and fasten off.

Lining (make 2)

Using 3mm needles and black, cast on 56 sts and work 2 rows st st.

Join in gold and work 2 rows st st.

Cont in 2-row stripe patt until 30 rows in all have been worked.

Shape top

Cont in stripe sequence, dec 4 sts on every knit row as folls:

Row 1: K10, skpo, k2tog, k28, k2tog, skpo, k10.

Row 2 and every alt row: Purl.

Row 3: K9, skpo, k2tog, k26, k2tog, skpo, k9.

Row 5: K8, skpo, k2tog, k24, k2tog, skpo, k8.

Cont as set until 16 sts rem.

Purl 1 row.

Cast off.

Making up

Assemble blossom, placing a small inner petal over a contrasting larger outer petal. Sew round base of cozy, interspersing leaves as desired. Using the length of yarn left on the outer petal, make 3 or 4 French knots in the centre of each flower. Sew in ends of yarn and ensure all bees are securely attached. Sew lining into cozy. Join side seams, leaving an opening for the handle and spout.

Who says tea cozies have to be boring? There's nothing traditional about this amazing felted creation by Rachel Proudman, so get out your needles and walk on the wild side.

Funky punk

Materials

Elle Merino Solids (76yds/70m per 50g ball)
2 x 50g balls shade 17 black (M)
Cascade 220 Heathers DK (220yds/201m per 100g ball)
1 x 50g ball 2426 red
1 x 50g ball 7825 orange
A pair of 6mm (US10:UK4) bamboo needles

Special techniques

Garter stitch
Stocking stitch
Wrap and turn (W&T): yf, sl next st k-wise, turn. Place sl st back on to R needle. On foll rows, knit wrap and sl st tog

Tension

Elle Merino: approx 15 sts to 9 cm and 15 rows to 7cm after felting
Cascade tension not crucial

Note: the cozy sides are sewn together before felting. Spikes are made from a triangle shape formed using short row shaping, and are attached before felting.

Cozy (make 2)

Using M and 6mm needles, cast on 40 sts and work 5 rows g-st.
Beg with a knit row, work 25 rows st st.

Shape top

Row 1: *K6 k2tog, rep from * to end (35 sts).

Next and every alt row: Purl.

Row 3: Knit.

Row 5: *k5 k2tog, rep from * to end (30 sts).

Row 7: Knit.

Row 9: *k4 k2tog, rep from * to end (25 sts).

Row 11: Knit.

Row 13: *k3, k2tog, rep from * to end (20 sts).

Row 15: *k2, k2tog, rep from * to end (15 sts).

Row 17: *k1, k2tog, rep from * to end (10 sts).

Row 19: *k2tog, rep from * to end (5 sts).

Row 20: Purl

Break off yarn and thread through rem sts. Draw up and fasten off.

Making up

Join back and front down both sides, leaving holes for the spout and handle.

Spikes

(make 5 red and 5 orange)

Cast on 13 sts.

Row 1: K11, W&T.

Row 2 and every alt row: Purl to end.

Row 3: K9, W&T.

Row 5: K7, W&T.

Row 7: K5, W&T.

Row 9: K4, W&T.

Row 11: K3, W&T.

Row 12: K2, W&T.

Row 13: K1, W&T.

Row 15: Knit across all sts, picking up the loops below the slipped sts and knitting them with the slipped sts.
Cast off all 13 sts.
Roll each triangle round to form a cone (the stitches will run round the cone and it will be a bit wiggly, but this does not matter. Attach cones to cozy along top seam and under handle by stitching round the base of each cone.

Felting

Place the cozy in a washing machine with a small amount of washing powder and a heavy item such as a pair of jeans or a bath towel – this will provide the friction necessary for the felting to take place. Run through a full cycle at 40°C to felt. Stretch into shape straight after washing and pull the spikes straight. Place on the teapot and dry in a warm place to keep the shape.

Tip

The washing process can be repeated if you feel that the cozy has not felted sufficiently.

This quirky design by Nicola Styliancu is worked in a pretty feather and fan pattern, and is guaranteed to bring a smile to your face at any time of day.

Octopus

Materials

Sirdar Snuggly DK (191 yds/175m per 50g ball)
1 x 50g ball 0392 Party Mix Pink (A)
Sirdar Snuggly Pearls DK
1 x 50g ball 0302 Pearly Pink (B)
A pair of 3.25mm (US3:UK10) needles
A set of 3.25mm (US3:UK10) double-pointed needles
1 x large black buttons
Oddment of red yarn
Stuffing

Special techniques

Feather and fan pattern (see instructions)

Tension

One rep of patt measures just over 6¼in (16cm) in width.

Legs (make 4 in each colour)

Using double-pointed needles, cast on 1 st.

Row 1: Knit into each st twice (2 sts).

Row 2: Push the 2 sts to the end of the needle. RS still facing k1, m1, k1.

Row 3: Push the 2 sts to the end of the needle. RS still facing k2, m1, k1.

Row 4: Push the 2 sts to the end of the needle. With RS still facing k3, m1, k1.

Row/round 5: K2 on to first dpn, k2 on to second dpn, k into final st twice using the third dpm. Place a marker after the sts on the third needle.

Round 6: Knit.

Round 7: K1, m1, k1 on needle 1, knit rest of round.

Round 8: K3, k1, m1, k1 on needle 2, knit rem sts.

Round 9: K6, k1, m1, k1 on needle 3.

Round 10: K2, m1, k1 on needle 1, knit rem sts.

Round 11: K4, k2, m1, k1 on needle 2, knit rem sts.

Round 12: K8, k2, m1, k1 on needle 3. Cont in this way, inc 1 st on each round, until there are 36 sts in total. Work in rounds without dec until leg measures 5in (13cm).

Finishing legs

Slip 6 sts from the middle needle on to each of the other needles. Stuff leg lightly. Hold the two needles parallel and, taking 1 st from each needle, k2tog across row. Place rem sts on a holder.

Body (make 2)

Using the 3.25mmm needles and A, cast on 74 sts and work in feather and fan pattern throughout the body.

Feather and fan pattern

Row 1 (RS): Using A, knit.

Row 2: Purl.

Row 3: K1, *(k2tog) 3 times, (yo, k1) 6 times, (k2tog) 3 times; rep from * to last st, k1.

Row 4: Knit.

These 4 rows form patt.

Grafting on the legs

Row 5: Using B, k1, then foll the k2tog method used to seal the legs, *(graft a light pink leg to work over foll 18 sts; graft a dark pink leg to work over the next 18 sts) rep from * to last st, k1.

Row 6: Purl.

Row 7: K1, *(k2tog) 3 times, (yo, k1) 4 times, (k2tog) 3 times; rep from * to last st, k1.

Row 8: Knit.

Beg with row 1, rep the feather and fan patt, changing cols as appropriate and ending with a 4th row, until work measures just over 5in (13cm).

Shape top

Row 1 (RS): Purl.

Row 2: Knit.

Row 3: K1, *(k2tog) 3 times, k1, (yo, k1) 4 times, (k2tog) 3 times; rep from * to end.

Row 4: Purl.

Row 5: Knit.

Row 6: Purl.

Row 7: K1, *(k2 tog) 3 times, (yo, k1) 4 times. (k2tog) 3 times; rep from * to last st, k1.

Row 8: Purl.

Row 9: Knit.

Row 10: Purl.

Row 11: K1, *(K2tog) 3 times, (yo, k1) twice, (k2tog) 3 times; rep from * to last st, k1.

Row 12: Purl.

Row 13: Knit.

Row 14: Purl.

Row 15: K1, *(k2tog) twice, (yo, k1) twice, (k2tog) twice; rep from * to end.

Row 16: Purl.

Row 17: Cont with colour from the previous row, k2tog to end.

Cast off.

Making up

Press the two sides, avoiding the legs. Join, leaving gaps for spout and handle. Attach the buttons to one side at the point where decs began. Using red yarn, chain stitch the mouth.

A *naked teapot!*

Techniques

How to make your prized pot decent

Measurements

The instructions given are for a standard six-cup teapot as shown. If your teapot is a little larger than this, try changing the needles for a bigger size and working a few more rows to make the sides longer. If it is smaller, a change to smaller needles may bring down the dimensions sufficiently.

Tension

Tension is important as just a slight difference can have a noticeable effect on the size of the finished cozy. If you are a new knitter, it is a good idea to start a habit that will save a lot of time in the end: work a swatch using the chosen yarn and needles. These can be labelled and filed for future reference. The tension required is given at the beginning of each pattern.

Materials and equipment

Needles and hooks

Most of the designs in this book are worked back and forth on standard knitting needles. Bamboo needles are useful if you are using a rough-textured yarn as they are very smooth and will help to prevent snags. You may also need double-pointed needles.

Where crochet hooks are used, these are standard metal hooks that are widely available.

Yarn

Cozies may be made in a huge variety of yarns. Wool or wool-mix yarns have the best insulating properties, but cotton or silk are also good. If you are using acrylic yarn, you may prefer to choose one of the thicker designs, or one that has a lining. Cozies are also an ideal way to use up oddments of yarn.

Substituting yarn

It is relatively simple to substitute different yarns for any of the projects in this book. One way to do this is to work out how many wraps per inch (wpi) the yarn produces (see table left). It is important to check tension, so begin by working a tension swatch. Then wind the yarn closely, in a single layer, round a rule or similar object, and count how many 'wraps' it produces to an inch (2.5cm). For a successful result, choose a yarn that produces twice, or slightly more than twice, the number of wraps per inch as there are stitches per inch in the tension swatch.

Tension required	Number of wraps per inch produced by yarn
8 sts per in (4-ply/fingering)	16–18 wraps per inch
6.5 sts per in (DK/sport)	13–14 wraps per inch
5.5 sts per in (Chunky/worsted)	11–12 wraps per inch

Knitting techniques

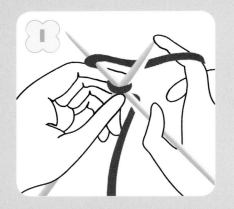  

Simple cast-on

 Form a slip knot on the left needle. Insert the right needle into the loop and wrap yarn round it as shown.

2 Pull the yarn through the first loop to create a new one.

3 Slide it on to the left-hand needle.

There are now 2 sts on the left needle. Continue in this way until you have the required number of sts.

Cable cast-on

For a firmer edge, cast on the first 2 sts as shown above. When casting on the third and subsequent sts, insert the needle *between* the cast-on sts on the left needle, wrap the yarn round and pull through to create a loop. Slide the loop on to the left needle. Repeat to end.

Thumb method cast-on

1 Make a slip knot some way from the end of the yarn and place on the needle. Pull the knot tight.

2 Hold needle in right hand and wrap the loose tail end round the left thumb, from front to back. Push the needle point through the thumb loop from front to back. Wind ball end of yarn round needle from left to right.

3 Pull the loop through thumb loop, then remove thumb. Gently pull the new loop tight using the tail yarn. Rep until the desired number of sts are on the needle.

Knit stitch

1 Hold the needle with the cast-on sts in your left hand. Place the tip of the empty right needle into the first st and wrap the yarn round as for casting on.

2 Pull the yarn through to create a new loop.

3 Slip the newly-made st on to the right needle.

Continue in the same way for each st on the left-hand needle.

To start a new row, turn the work to swap the needles and repeat steps.

Purl stitch

1 Hold the yarn at the front of the work as shown.

2 Place the right needle into the first st from front to back. Wrap the yarn round the needle in an anti-clockwise direction as shown.

3 Bring the needle back through the st and pull through.

Ⓐ Garter stitch (g-st)

Knit every row.

Ⓑ Stocking stitch (st st)

Knit on RS rows and purl on WS rows.

Ⓒ Moss stitch (m-st)

With an even number of sts:
Row 1: (k1, p1) to end.
Row 2: (p1, k1) to end.
Rep rows 1 and 2 for pattern.

With an odd number of sts:
Row 1: * k1, p1, rep from * to
last st, k1.
Rep to form pattern.

Ⓓ Single (1 x 1) rib

With an even number of sts:
Row 1: *K1, p1* rep to end.
Rep for each row.

With an odd number of sts:
Row 1: *K1, p1, rep from * to
last st, k1.
Row 2: *P1, k1, rep from * to
last st, p1.

Ⓔ Double (2 x 2) rib

Row 1: *K2, p2, rep from * to end.
Rep for each row.

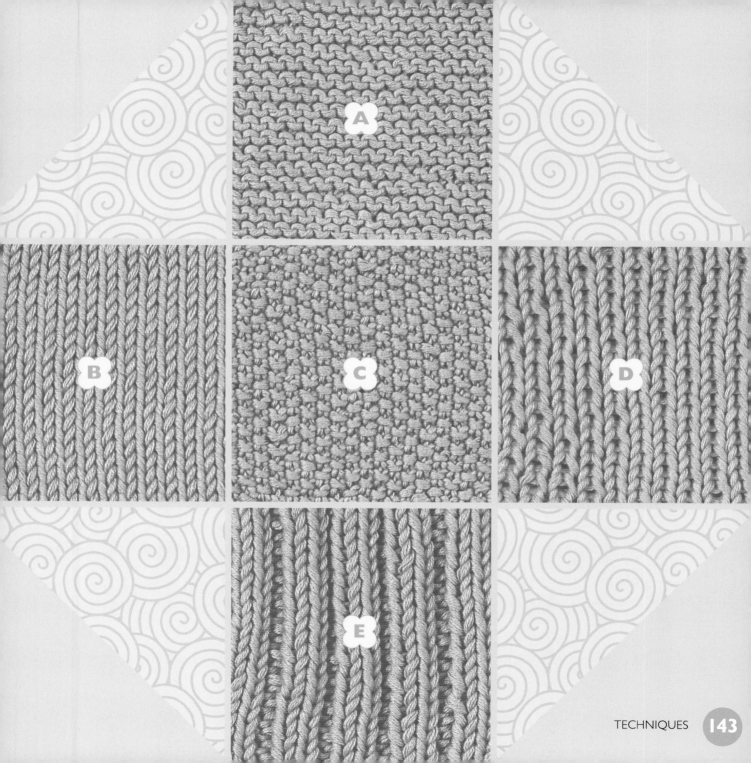

Cable stitch

With the help of a cable needle, these decorative stitches are quite straightforward. Stitches are slipped on to the needle and then knitted later to create the twists.

Front cable worked over 4 sts (cab4f)

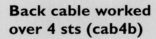 Slip the next 2 sts on to a cable needle and hold in front of work.

2 Knit the next 2 stitches from the left needle as normal, then knit the 2 sts from the cable needle.

Back cable worked over 4 sts (cab4b)

Slip the next 2 sts on to a cable needle and hold at back of work.

Knit the next 2 sts from the left needle as normal, then knit the 2 sts from the cable needle.

Colour knitting

Fairisle

Fairisle uses the stranding technique, which involves picking up and dropping yarns as they are needed. Yarns are then carried across the row and loops formed at the back of the work. These should not exceed about 5 sts in length. Make sure the tension of loops is even or the fabric may pucker.

1 Begin knitting with the first colour (A) and drop it when you need to incorporate the second (B). To pick up A again bring it under B and knit again.

2 To pick up B again, drop A and bring B over A, then knit again.

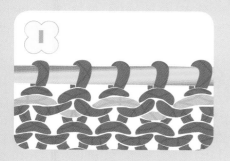

Reading charts

Most charts are shown in squares, with each square representing a stitch. They are usually marked in sections of ten stitches, which makes counting easier. When working in stocking stitch on straight needles, read the chart from right to left on knit (RS) rows and from left to right on purl (WS) rows. Check carefully after every purl row to make sure the pattern stitches are in the correct place.

Intarsia

Blocks of colour are created by using the intarsia technique of twisting the yarns together at the back of the work with each colour change (see diagram above). It is better to use bobbins than whole balls to prevent tangling. They are smaller and can hang at the back of the work out of the way. Once finished, ends are woven in at the back, and pressing under a damp cloth will help to neaten any distorted stitches.

Finishing off

Casting off

1 Knit 2 sts on to the right needle, then slip the first st over the second st and let it drop off the needle (1 st remains).

2 Knit another st so you have 2 sts on the right needle again.

Rep process until there is only 1 st on the left needle. Break yarn and thread through rem st to fasten off.

Sewing up

Place the pieces to be joined on a flat surface laid together side-by-side with right sides towards you. Using matching yarn, thread a needle back and forth with small, straight stitches. The stitches form a ladder between the two pieces of fabric, creating a flat, secure seam. This technique is usually known as mattress stitch.

Stocking stitch joins

The edges of stocking stitch tend to curl, so it may be tricky to join. The best way to join it is to use mattress stitch to pick up the bars between the columns of stitches.

Working upwards or downwards according to preference, secure the yarn to one of the pieces you want to join. Place the edges of the work together and pick up a bar from one side, then pick up the corresponding bar from the opposite side. Repeat. After a few stitches, pull gently on the yarn and the two sides will come together in a seam that is almost invisible. Take care to stay in the same column all the way. Do not pull the stitches tight at first as you will not be able to see what you are doing.

Garter stitch joins

It is easier to join garter stitch as it has a firm edge and lies flat. Place the edges of the work together, right side up, and see where the stitches line up. Pick up the bottom loops of the stitches on one side of the work and the top loops of the stitches on the other side. After a few stitches, pull gently on the yarn. The stitches should lock together and lie completely flat. The inside of the join should look the same as it does on the outside.

Crochet techniques

Chain stitch (ch)

1 With hook in right hand and yarn resting over middle finger of left hand, pull yarn taut. Take hook under, then over yarn.

2 Pull the hook and yarn through the loop while holding slip knot steady. Rep to form a foundation row of chain stitch (ch).

Double crochet (dc)

1 Place hook into a st. Wrap yarn round hook and draw the loop back through the work towards you.

2 There should now be two loops on the hook. Wrap yarn round hook again, then draw through both loops, leaving one loop on the hook (one double crochet (dc) now complete. Rep to continue row.

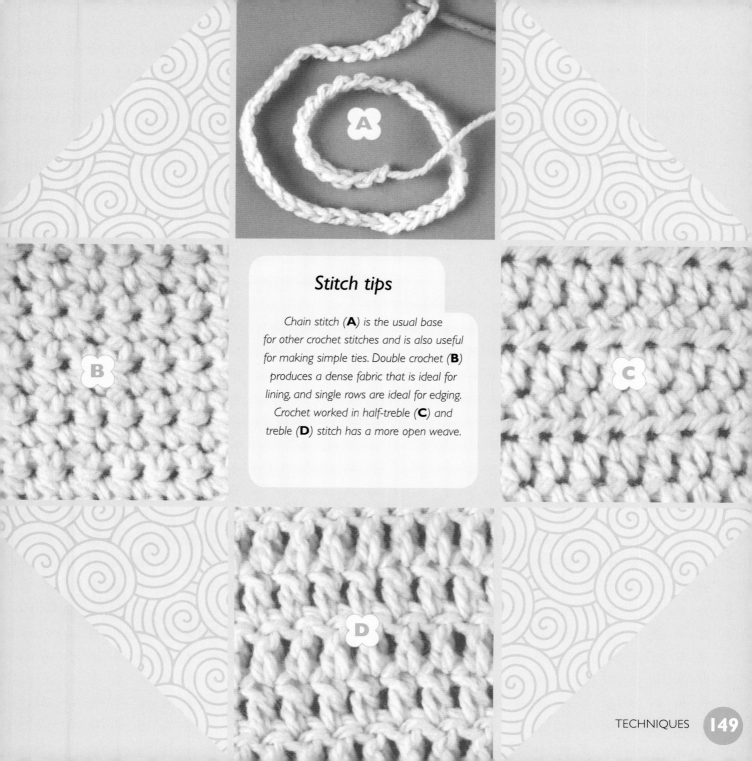

Stitch tips

Chain stitch (**A**) is the usual base for other crochet stitches and is also useful for making simple ties. Double crochet (**B**) produces a dense fabric that is ideal for lining, and single rows are ideal for edging. Crochet worked in half-treble (**C**) and treble (**D**) stitch has a more open weave.

Half-treble (h-tr)

Wrap yarn round hook, then place into a stitch. Wrap yarn round hook, then draw the loop through (3 loops now on hook). Wrap yarn round hook again and draw through the 3 loops (one loop remains on hook).

Treble (tr)

Follow instructions for half treble until there are 3 loops on the hook. Catch yarn with hook and draw through 2 of the loops, then catch yarn again and draw through rem 2 loops.

Finishing touches

Blanket stitch

Work from left to right. The twisted edge should lie on the outer edge of the fabric to form a raised line. Bring needle up at point **A**, down at **B** and up at **C** with thread looped under the needle. Pull through. Take care to tighten the stitches equally. Repeat to the right. Fasten the last loop by taking a small stitch along the lower line.

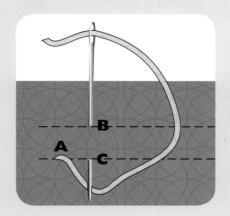
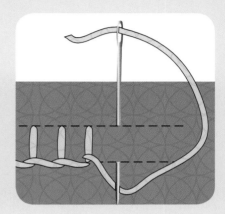

French knots

Work in any direction.

1 Bring needle to RS of fabric. Holding thread taut with finger and thumb of left hand, wind thread once or twice around needle tip.

2 Still holding thread, insert needle tip close to the point where you brought the needle out to the RS of work and pull needle to back so that the twist lies neatly on the fabric surface. Repeat as required.

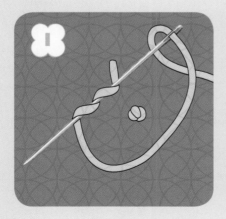
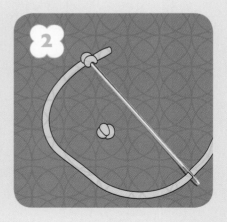

Making pompons

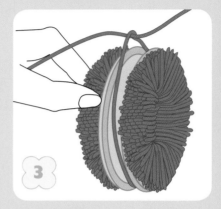

1 Cut out two cardboard circles a little smaller in diameter than the pompon you want. Make a hole in the middle of both about a third of the diameter. Put both circles together and using lengths of yarn, thread through the middle and begin wrapping around the outer edge until your card is completely covered. Use one or more colours for different effects. Continue working in this way until the centre hole is only a pinprick.

2 With sharp-ended scissors, cut all around the edge of the circle, slicing through all the strands of yarn.

3 Now ease a length of yarn between the card discs and tie very firmly around the centre, leaving a tail for sewing. You have now secured all the strands of yarn around the middle. Ease the card discs away from the pompon and fluff out all the strands. Trim off any loose or straggly ends.

Making an I-cord

Using double-pointed needles, cast on the required number of stitches. Do not turn; slide stiches to the opposite end of the needle, then take the yarn firmly across the back of work. Knit stitches again. Repeat to desired length. Cast off.

Abbreviations

approx	approximately
beg	beginning
C	contrast (colour)
ch	chain stitch
cm(s)	centimetre(s)
cont	continue
corresp	corresponding
dc	double crochet
dec	decrease
d-g st	double garter stitch (2 rounds p, 2 rounds k)
DK	double knitting
foll	following
g	gramme(s)
g-st	garter stitch
htr	half treble
in(s)	inch(es)
inc	increase by working twice into the stitch
K/k	knit
k-wise	knitwise, as if to knit
k1 tbl	knit 1 st through the back of the loop
k2tog	knit 2 sts together
L	left

LH	left-hand side
m	metre
M	main (colour)
M1	make 1 stitch
M1L	make 1 stitch slanting left (left increase)
M1R	make 1 stitch slanting right (right increase)
mm	millimetres
m-st	moss stitch
P/p	purl
patt	pattern
p2tog	purl two stitches together
psso	pass slipped stitch over
p-wise	purlwise, as if to purl
rem	remaining
rev st st	reverse stocking stitch
R	right
RS	right side of work
sk	skip
skpo	slip 1 st, k 1 st, pass slipped st over
sl	slip
ss	slip stitch

ssk	slip 1 st k-wise, slip 1 st p-wise; knit these 2 sts together through the back of the loops
ssp	slip 1 st knitwise, slip 1 stitch purlwise, then purl both stitches together
st(s)	stitch(es)
st st	stocking stitch
T3L	twist 3 sts left
t-ch	turning chain
tog	together
tr	treble
WS	wrong side of work
yb	yarn back
yd(s)	yard (s)
yf	yarn forward
yo	yarn over needle
WS	wrong side of work
*	work instructions following *, then repeat as directed
( )	repeat instructions inside brackets as directed

Conversions

Needle sizes

UK	Metric	US
14	2mm	0
13	2.5mm	1
12	2.75mm	2
11	3mm	–
10	3.25mm	3
–	3.5mm	4
9	3.75mm	5
8	4mm	6
7	4.5mm	7
6	5mm	8
5	5.5mm	9
4	6mm	10
3	6.5mm	10.5
2	7mm	10.5
1	7.5mm	11
0	8mm	11
00	9mm	13
000	10mm	15

UK/US yarn weights

UK	US
2–ply	Lace
3–ply	Fingering
4–ply	Sport
Double knitting	Light worsted
Aran	Fisherman/worsted
Chunky	Bulky
Super chunky	Extra bulky

GMC Publications would like to thank the following people for their help in supplying props and locations for this book: Jane Kaufman, Emma Foster, Alison Howard, Gilda Pacitti.

Index

To place an order, or to request a catalogue, contact:

GMC Publications Ltd

Castle Place, 166 High Street, Lewes, East Sussex, BN7 1XU

United Kingdom

Tel: 01273 488005   **Fax:** 01273 402866

Website: www.gmcbooks.com

Orders by credit card are accepted